Greatness Guide 2

A Coaching Manual for

Managers in the

Low Voltage Systems Industry

Andy Bernot

In memory of John Ford

He loved his team and led them to greatness

He made his mark and left an enviable legacy

Acknowledgements

My sincere thanks to all the managers that I worked with during my career, all of you have provided me with insights that shaped my philosophy that guided my decisions and actions.

Secondly, I offer both my gratitude and apologies to the colleagues I had the opportunity to manage and lead. Reflecting upon my journey I share a common human pain, I wish I knew then what I know now. Thank you for the privilege to lead. You provided me with opportunity to learn and grow as a leader.

Table of Contents

Introduction

Congratulations! You have a phenomenal opportunity to achieve personal greatness. You also can help your team to achieve their greatness. As manager you have vast control over many resources and decisions. You have positional power, but you do not have the role of dictator. Rather the manager has essential roles and responsibilities that if performed with passion and competency will result in energized colleagues that will create satisfied customers who will reward the business with profitable growth.

Some of the key roles you play include:

- **Leader:** You set the tone for your organization. Colleagues look to you for direction, support and feedback. Your words and actions play the critical role in the development of culture.
- **Coach:** As coach you prepare your team to compete and win in the marketplace. You establish routines, you teach, you lead practice and you call plays. You hold the team accountable for their assignments. You assess performance and you make adjustments.
- **Strategist:** You are the master planner. You facilitate the alignment of individual team member's thinking in order to achieve goals. In this role you determine priorities and focus.
- **Motivator:** You keep the team energized and focused on the mission. The success of the organization is the result of the collective success of each colleague.

- **Visionary:** You paint the picture of the future state you are leading the organization toward. You communicate mission and purpose to the colleagues. You help connect the dots for the team that excites them to join your journey.
- **Face of the organization:** You embody professionalism, commitment and excellence. The community looks to you for assurance and confidence.

Some of your key responsibilities include:

- **Delivering Results:** You are accountable to deliver financial performance results. Revenue growth, profitability and cash flow management are essential. Secondary metrics are often assigned as goals by leadership that has strategic importance.
- **Leading change:** The quote "What got us here won't get us there" underscores the imperative to change what you do and how you do it. You are responsible to define and communicate the current state and the future state. You are the catalyst for organizational change that is necessary for growth.
- **Developing your team:** Each colleague is accountable for his or her personal development. You are responsible for developing your team. For your team to develop they must understand your vision, mission and strategy. Then they must collaborate with team members to build trust. Teams must evolve through the stages of organizational

development of; form, storm, norm and perform.

- **Caring for customers and colleagues**: You are directly responsible for the care of your colleagues. Additionally, you are responsible for the care of all customers. It is understood that your colleagues have significantly more customer facing time than yourself but it is through your care and passion with colleagues that care of customers is manifested.
- **Building positive culture:** Organizational culture is evolving continually. It is the result of millions of actions from each colleague occurring over time. You are the critical factor in guiding and shaping culture. You set the tone and pace. What you acknowledge and praise will be amplified. What you reprimand and challenge will be minimized.

It is helpful to think of your key role as the owner of your operation as opposed to a caretaker of the business. And remember the relevant mantra "if it is to be, it is up to me".

The Greatness Guide

This manual has been developed to guide you in your quest to achieve greatness as a manager. I can assure you that your quest is a noble one and will not be accomplished without much toil and persistence. Like any endeavor in life you must go through natural stages of progression. At one point in time we are all rookie managers. We are knighted and are given the opportunity and responsibility to lead a team of colleagues.

The fact that you have earned the position as manager and leader of your business unit suggests that you have already demonstrated a high level of competency in your previous endeavors. Historically, new managers rise through the ranks within the low voltage industry. They demonstrate excellence in their previous assignments as individual contributors. Their excellence is recognized by the organization. Consequently, excellence is rewarded with promotion to greater responsibility.

The skills, knowledge and attitudes that you developed to this point in your career will remain your foundation. As you move forward in your managerial career the principles that resulted in your previous success will be useful for you and your team. Additionally, you must remain attentive to new knowledge that will advance your thinking. Furthermore you must experiment with new ideas for knowledge without application equals nothing.

This coaching manual is packed with practical knowledge that will be absolutely useful in your quest to achieve organizational greatness. This manual will also provide work tools, tips, recommendations and models for your benefit. But essentially the success you experience will be the direct result of how you interpret and apply the information you acquire.

In his book *"The Law of Success"* Napoleon Hill believes that individuals must identify their definite chief aim in life.[1] Extending that thought into your career decision, what is your definite chief aim? Are you committed to building the greatest organization the industry has ever imagined?

---

[1] Napoleon Hill, *The Law of Success*, (The Penguin Group, New York, 1928)

Transformation Model

Building your business and achieving organizational greatness is a marathon effort filled with complexity but the model for transformation is simple. Consider the following as to how individuals and organizations learn, grow and transform.

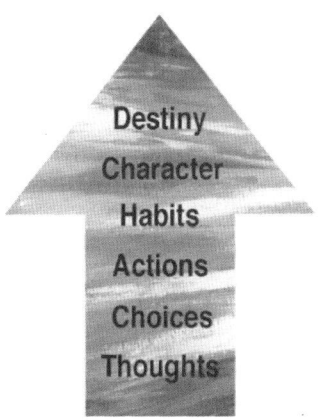

This guide intends to affect your thinking about how you manage and lead your organization. With those thoughts you will make **Choices,** internalize information and determine what you will accept. **Action** is the next critical step, and clearly, knowledge without action results in nothing. Your purposeful actions will determine your success.

As you see the positive effects of your actions you will repeat them thereby developing the **Habits** that will improve your efficiency and effectiveness. Your belief and discipline to your habits will develop your personal leadership qualities that define your **Character.** As your team witnesses the results of your leadership they will adopt your values and beliefs and mirror your practices. As more colleagues engage in your transformation model, culture will strengthen and organizational greatness will be the result.

You cannot achieve organizational greatness through your efforts alone. But you do play the critical role of Architect. You define the vision, mission and strategy. You are the catalyst for energizing your colleagues and inspiring them to achieve personal greatness.

What is Personal Greatness?

Personal greatness is realizing a person's full potential as a professional and as a human. Realizing full potential is simple in concept, but it is not easy. In my view achieving personal greatness can be defined in five aspects: effort, principles, growth, service and delivering results.

Max Effort: How does it feel when you know you have given your absolute best effort? Do you have a sense of pride? Do you have integrity? Others may motivate you, but you are the only one who knows if you have applied maximum effort. Most people, when being objective, acknowledge that maximum effort is rarely applied. Your absolute best efforts are a key element in achieving personal greatness.

Hero Principles: What is your image of Hero Principles? Think about the people you personally hold in highest regard as well as history's great leaders. Hero Principles include integrity, courage, accountability, humility, compassion and generosity. You decide which principles resonate most with you. The second element of achieving personal greatness is consistently living Hero Principles every day.

Personal Growth: The expression "What got you here, won't get you there" is appropriate when discussing the prospect of achieving personal greatness. Regardless of your current skill set, you can and must get better. Although personal growth happens naturally from day to day experiences, individuals who aspire to achieve personal greatness realize the need to be intentional about their personal growth. They have a plan and they set goals for themselves that makes them more valuable.

Serve Others: The next element in achieving personal greatness is the passion and excellence in which you serve others. The list of others includes clients, peers, supervisors and community stakeholders. When applying your maximum effort with noble principles for the benefit of others you are demonstrating personal leadership. As you intentionally learn and grow you expand your excellence in serving the world and consequently move closer to achieving your full potential.

Deliver Results: It would be logical to see how the combination of effort, principles, improvement and service would result in great success. But life is not always logical on a timeline. The final aspect of achieving personal greatness is winning, that is, delivering results. Achieving both your financial and non-financial goals and objectives.

Achieve Organizational Greatness

An organization is the sum total of its parts. Consequently the leader understands that the organization is only as strong as the weakest link. To achieve organizational greatness the leader must be mindful of the needs of the colleagues. The leader cannot go it alone. Achieving organizational greatness requires a team of energized colleagues who embrace your vision and willingly join your journey.

The Formula

The challenge ahead of you will be complex and will often have you scratching your head on a course of action. This coaching manual attempts to provide you with a formula to achieve organizational greatness.

The first element of the formula is building your leadership foundation. Welcome to section one.

Section 1 - Build Your Leadership Foundation

Personal Leadership

The objective of this manual is to guide you on your journey towards achieving organizational greatness. The first section of this book is focused on your leadership foundation. The first chapter in leadership foundation is personal leadership.

Here is a question: Is there a difference between <u>personal leadership and leadership</u>? The question is posed so as to stimulate reflection on how you lead yourself versus how you lead others. In my view, before you can effectively lead an organization to greatness, you must first lead yourself to greatness.

In the introduction of this book I defined personal greatness in five aspects, which are:

- Maximum effort
- Hero principles
- Personal growth
- Serve others
- Deliver results

I offer that personal leadership is the spark that awakens the desire within you to pursue achieving personal greatness.

In our professional lives we define leadership as the influencing of people by providing purpose, direction and motivation while operating to accomplish the goals and improving the organization.

In our personal lives we define leadership as the act of determining our life's purpose and direction, then accomplishing goals and continually improving ourselves.

What about the business of **YOU**? Have you defined your purpose and your "life's mission"?

The process of defining your life's mission starts by answering the key questions of:

- What do you want to be?
- What do you want to achieve?
- What principles do you want to possess and live by?

My Life's Mission – Key Questions	
What do I want to be? (Character)	•As parent, spouse, family member •As community member •As business leader and mentor •As friend and neighbor
What do I want to do? (Achievements or contributions)	•As parent, spouse, family member •As community member •As business leader and mentor •As friend and neighbor
What do I want to have? (Values or principles)	•As parent, spouse, family member •As community member •As business leader and mentor •As friend and neighbor

Defining and guiding your life's mission is personal. Only you know what is right for you. It starts with your spirit, your inner voice that guides you to the things that matter most to you. In his book *The 8th Habit* [2], Steven Covey provides a model of how he defines and guides personal

[2] Steven R. Covey, *The 8th Habit, (Simon & Schuster, New York, 2004)*

mission. The better you become at expanding these human capacities the greater your life becomes:

- **Conscience:** The guiding force to vision, discipline and passion.
- **Vision:** Seeing with your mind's eye the possibilities in your life.
- **Discipline:** Paying the price to bring that vision into reality.
- **Passion:** The strength in conviction that sustains the discipline to achieve the vision.

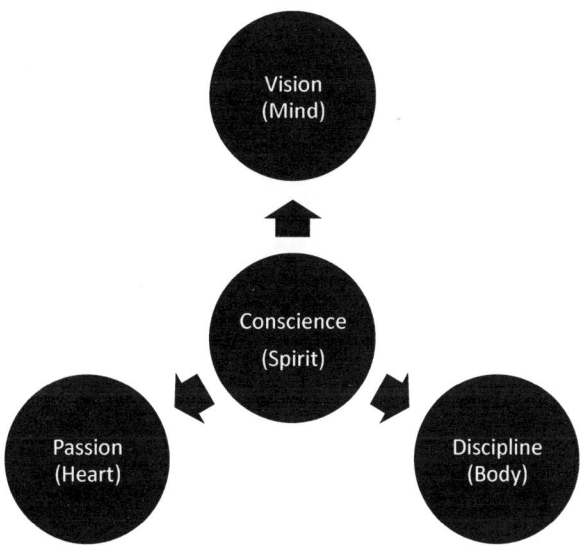

Personal leadership is a continuous journey. As your personal leadership develops, your vision of your life's possibilities expands. As you enjoy victories in life, your discipline is further strengthened, and your passion grows. As your passion grows, you enjoy greater victories and you see greater possibilities causing your vision to evolve.

Defining your life's mission and vision is but one aspect of personal leadership. But it is one of the most impactful and clarifying things you can and should do.

A helpful guide for developing your mission is Steven Covey's book *The 7 Habits of Highly Effective People.*[3] Habit 2; Begin With the End in Mind, asks you to think about your life's mission by considering your own funeral as an observer and to hear the way family, friends and community reflect upon your life and the impact you have had on them.

Remember, before you can lead others you must first lead yourself. Step 1; define your life's mission.

---

[3] Steven R. Covey, *The 7 Habits of Highly Effective People, (Simon and Shuster, New York, 2004)*

Leadership Philosophy

Throughout this guide I reference leadership so much that you will clearly understand that it is the most critical factor in achieving both your personal success and organizational success. But this thing we call leadership is mysterious in its attainment. Most managers aspire to become a great leader, not all attain it. The author Og Mandino is credited with this quote on leadership; "It is easier for one who is to be than for someone who is not to become".

There are many discussions about whether leaders are born with the magical leadership gene or if it is a learned competency. The fact that I am writing about this subject in a coaching manual should expose that I believe leadership is a competency that can be developed.

In 1948 a study was conducted to determine the key principles of leadership and the findings summarized 11 points.[4] When you review each of these points consider how you rank yourself. If you rank below excellent in any of these points ask how would you go about improving your competency?

- Know yourself and seek self-improvement
- Be technically proficient
- Seek responsibility and take responsibility for your actions
- Set the example
- Know your people and look out for their welfare
- Keep your people informed

---

[4] Ed Ruggero, Dennis F. Haley, *The Leader's Compass, (Academy Leadership, King of Prussia, PA, 2005)*

- Ensure that the task is understood, supervised and accomplished
- Develop a sense of responsibility among your people
- Train your people as a team
- Make sound and timely decisions
- Employ your work unit in accordance with its capabilities

Leadership is influencing people by providing purpose, direction and motivation while operating to accomplish the goals and improving the organization. Last chapter I clarified that personal leadership is about leading yourself. In your role as manager you are leading others through your influence upon them. What are of the key behaviors of people who have had a positive influence on you?

A survey conducted to determine what colleagues expect of leaders resulted in the following:[5]

- Honest, just and fair treatment
- Consideration of them as mature professional workers
- The opportunity to work within a climate of trust and confidence
- Acceptance of errors and the opportunity to use them as learning experiences
- Personal interest taken in them as individuals
- Loyalty
- Shielding from harassment from higher ups
- Anticipating and meeting their needs
- Being told the purpose of tasks
- Clear-cut and positive decisions and instructions that are not constantly changing

---

[5] Ed Ruggero, Dennis F. Haley, *The Leader's Compass*, (Academy Leadership, King of Prussia, PA, 2005)

These colleague expectations look reasonable. As the leader you should know the reasonable expectations of your colleagues and live up to their expectations. Additionally, you must establish your expectations of the colleagues and manage them accordingly.

Developing your Leadership Philosophy

A number of years ago I participated in a workshop that provided insight on the value of having a leadership philosophy. I give credit to the presenter Ed Ruggero and his book titled "The Leader's Compass" for enlightening me on the value of developing and using a leadership philosophy.

I don't doubt that you have a leadership philosophy. Have you written it down? Most managers have leadership beliefs, but few have condensed their beliefs to writing. The exercise of writing and then sharing your leadership philosophy will strengthen you and your organization.

These are the key questions that must be addressed:

- What are my values and beliefs?
- What can colleagues expect from me?
- What do I expect from colleagues?
- What are my non-negotiables?

What are my values and beliefs: When you tell your team what your values and beliefs are you bring clarity and confidence to the team. This is beneficial in building trust. Trust is essential in building a winning culture.

Defining your values and beliefs can result in an extensive list so you need to use good judgment on how granular you get. Stating your top ten or so seems to work well.

One exercise that helps is to think about your best boss and list their most favorable behaviors. Then do the exercise for the worst boss and list their most unfavorable behaviors. This exercise will help you clarify the values and beliefs that you hold dear.

What colleagues can expect from me? This is an accountability statement and a promise to be consistent in your behavior. You also give permission to colleagues to remind you when you behave inconsistent with your words.

What I expect from colleagues: This list of expectations takes away any uncertainty. Colleagues now clearly know what they must do to flourish within the organization. This becomes their accountability statement, their promise.

My non-negotiables? These are the list of behaviors that will lead a colleague to termination. These behaviors are related to ethical or legal conduct. Some examples include physical harassment, verbal harassment, physical violence, lying and theft. You determine what your non-negotiables are. Although they may seem obvious they are certainties and they are powerful.

I recommended that you share your leadership philosophy with a trusted peer and request their feedback. Many times others observe leadership behaviors in you that you may have overlooked.

Once you feel that your leadership philosophy represents you accurately you will be well served by using it in several forums:

- Introduction to the new team: You can imagine the first impression you make on your team when you present your leadership philosophy. It is memorable.
- Share it with new colleagues as part of on boarding.

- Share it with job candidates as an indicator of culture.
- Share it with new managers and supervisors as an example of what they should create.
- Post it in your office for the colleagues to see.

I highly recommend you write your leadership philosophy and share it with your team. Also, I suggest reading The Leader's Compass by Ed Ruggero for practical applications and examples.

Core Values

As a new manager you are under the microscope. Everyone is curious about the new boss. Your colleagues will be evaluating and interpreting every move you make and every word you state. You have a unique opportunity to shape the minds of your team by sharing your core values and beliefs.

What are your core values and beliefs? If you are like most managers you know the answer but you may not have condensed it to writing. The same is true for many organizations. This is the reason why organizations have applied great effort to determine their core values and beliefs. They came to realize the inherent power of clarifying their vision, mission and values.

Clarifying your core values is the first part of the success formula. The second step is for you to communicate why your core values are relevant in the achievement of your vision and mission. You interpret reality for your team.

If you are representing an organization that has defined core values you are responsible to embrace them and make them your own. Your team will be judging your authenticity toward the company's core values. Colleagues can sense if the leader truly believes and owns the core values or if it is lip service for the organization.

Why are values important?

- Your values guide your thoughts, words and actions.
- Your values help you to grow and develop.
- Your values help you to create the future you want.

- The decisions you make are a reflection of your values.
- Your values support your vision and mission.

Your team will be interested in your values and beliefs. Understandably each colleague will have their own set of values and beliefs. Your challenge is to align the core values of the team and to establish a set of shared values.

Shared values will help guide your business and colleagues in the right direction. Shared values guide how colleagues should behave, how work should be done and how colleagues should treat each other.

There are ample examples of core values that have been established by world-class organizations. A web search will provide you with many ideas. Most organizations see the wisdom of publishing a list of core values that is limited to the critical few. It would be hard to argue against any noble value, but emphasizing the "core values" aids in aligning and unifying the team through a focused on the critical few.

Integrity

Many organizations establish a code of standards, key principles or core values for the purpose of defining the culture they are aspiring to create. These efforts attempt to distill the many important principles of life into the critical few that are viewed as most important to the organization at a point in time. Not surprisingly, the core value of integrity continues to be on the list of most organizations. It seems evident that integrity is vital in every aspect of our lives and thus worthy to promote with rigor.

How do we measure integrity? Are there degrees of integrity or is it simply a yes/no answer? When we look at others can we determine integrity by their actions? When we evaluate organizations, do we judge their integrity by the actions of their members? Can individuals and organizations that have had lapses in integrity rebound in the opinions of the world? These questions highlight the fact that we are not perfect as individuals or as organizations.

You cannot achieve personal greatness without the consistent pursuit of living a life of integrity. This pursuit includes all dimensions of your life; business, family and community. Lack of integrity in one area will affect your life balance. As you practice integrity and consciously recognize your congruency, you become stronger and build your resolve to always be true to yourself and your commitment to integrity.

Only you know if you are acting with integrity. Others will develop an opinion about you and your integrity based on your words and actions, but over time the truth will become evident. I recall an interview where the speaker made a claim that shaped my perspective. The statement was "We measure others by their actions, we measure ourselves by our intentions." How do your intentions toward integrity compare with your actions? Thoughts matter, words matter, actions matter.

Here are some of the practical reminders of integrity within your role as a manager:

- Make and keep commitments.
- Be truthful with yourself and others.
- Be honest and transparent in communications.
- Think and deal in the best interests of colleagues.
- Think and deal in the best interests of customers.

- Treat everyone as the most important person in the world.
- Do not say anything about others in their absence that you would not say in their presence.
- Doing the right thing always leads to better results.
- Doing what is right leads to better relationships.
- Better relationships lead to bigger and better opportunities.
- Have the courage to say no.

Integrity is the central component of your leadership. The world is watching you and keeping score. The quote "What you are speaks so loudly that I can't hear a word you say" applies to integrity. Your team is playing off your queues. Your words supported by your actions will play a substantive role in building the culture of your organization. The expression "Do as I say, not as I do" has no home in your organization. You are the leader and leaders lead the way in both words and deeds.

Vision

The vision of the world's best organizations has something in common. They understand where they are going, how they are going to get there and what their Utopia will look like once they arrive. When a group of people have a shared vision of what they are building and believe strongly in the mission they are inspired, and they can see how their efforts contribute to the vision.

What is your vision? A simple question yet surprisingly most managers have not given the question serious thought. Jim Horan, the author of *The One Page Business Plan*[6] provides a useful set of questions to guide leaders in their quest to define or clarify their vision. These questions include:

- What type of business is this?
- What markets does it serve?
- What is the geographic scope?
- Who are the target customers?
- What are the key products and services?
- How big will the business be in 5 years?

Vision is the practice of seeing beyond the present reality. To create in the mind what does not currently exist in order to become something better in the future. In answering the questions above it is important to remember that your future state will be different than your current state. As you move toward your vision the answer to these questions will evolve year by year.

---

[6] Jim Horan, *The One Page Business Plan, Independently Published 1998*

The exercise of answering these questions will result in clarity of your vision. Your vision can be condensed to a vision statement, which is useful to your leadership team, colleagues and clients:

- **For Leadership**: the vision statement challenges the on-going evaluation of the markets being served and the products and services offered. The vision statement also guides the evaluation of financial investments and strategies to achieve growth.
- **For Colleagues**: the vision statement provides clarity of where the organization is going and inspires them to want to make meaningful contributions.
- **For Clients**: the vision statement will help them determine if the cultures are compatible and if the philosophies align.

A well-written vision statement answers the question "What is being built" in three sentences or less. It should describe what the business should look like in five years. An effective vision statement supports your efforts to build an energizing culture. Your vision statement should excite and motivate your team.

Unfortunately, your vision statement may not inspire all colleagues. This can be attributed to the way individuals interpret the Why behind the vision. The vision describes what is being built which can be referred to in dollars of growth over a period of years. This metric does not create excitement but with little imagination it becomes clear that financial growth is the catalyst for colleagues to grow into new positions, gain promotions and have challenging work.

You are the captain of your ship and you must understand where you are going and how you intend to get there. Communicate and reinforce your vision to the team. A leader without a vision is like a ship without a rudder, it is moving and reacting to nature's opportunities but it is not being guided to the destination.

Mission

Every business exists for a reason. Can you describe why your business exists? The business consultant, Simon Sinek, popularized the phrase "finding your <u>Why</u>" where he explains his revelation about high performing companies. In his view, history shows that companies and individuals who articulate <u>why</u> they do what they do attract like-minded people to join in their journey. He provides examples of Apple, Martin Luther King and the Wright Brothers as affirming success stories.

In your role as leader and visionary for your business you have the opportunity and responsibility to define meaning and purpose to your colleagues. You define "The Why". You connect the dots for colleagues to show how their individual roles and responsibilities align with the mission.

Defining your <u>why</u> starts with understanding who you intend to serve and what you will do for them. Consider facilitating a cross-functional team workshop to clarify your mission and create your mission statement.

There is no questioning the value of having a clear mission. Logically, a written mission statement provides value to the authors, the team and the customers. There are no parameters in writing a mission statement, but experience shows that the best mission statements are short, memorable and have an emotional element.

When creating a mission statement is viewed as a required exercise rather than a passionate exploration it will do more harm than good in building business momentum. Leaders intuitively understand that defining "The Why" is essential for the marathon they are embarking upon.

Be Proactive

As manager you have many responsibilities that you must attend to. The achievement of any objective can only be accomplished through your actions or the actions of those within your organization. But the key to managerial success is proactive rather than reactive management.

In his book, *The 7 Habits of Highly Effective People*, Steven Covey defines Habit 1 as "Be Proactive".[7] Covey defines proactivity as focusing on things that are important but not yet urgent. Examples of managerial activities that fit within this definition include:

- Planning
- Training
- Most one-on one meetings
- Most coaching sessions
- Many customer visits

Since your time is a finite resource you must use it effectively. Even with the best of intentions managers will be challenged with many requests that are not their desired priority. Some will be time wasters that must be minimized. Others may be opportunities that are important and urgent. All managers must develop the wisdom to determine which activities take priority.

Great managers operate with a sense of urgency. They attack the day and treat time as a precious resource. They are focused on working their plan and building

---

[7] Steven R. Covey, *The 7 Habits of Highly Effective People, (Simon and Schuster, New York, 2004)*

relationships with their team. They lead by example and consequently build a culture that respects time.

Priorities

When discussing the topic of priorities two quotes come to mind. "When everything is important, nothing is" and "You can do anything but you can't do everything".

As the manager of your operation you are responsible for the achievement of goals and objectives through the efforts of yourself and others. There is ever increasing complexity as your business continues to grow and prosper. Ultimately, your circumstances are changing and you and your team must adapt.

The challenge every person faces is discerning priorities. How does one determine what and where to invest their time and effort? Recognizing that time is a limited resources it is clear that you must carefully plan how you make the best use of your time. Again, you can do anything but you can't do everything. So the humbling reality is that your decisions will determine your destiny. So how do you determine priorities?

- **Be true to your vision and mission:** Are your priorities aligned and will they facilitate the achievement of your vision and mission?
- **Focus on colleagues:** Managers achieve organizational results through the efforts of others. To achieve superior results you must have superior people. If you do not have superior people you must develop them, reposition them or remove them. Colleague focused activities include coaching, group training sessions and performance feedback discussions.

- **Focus on customers:** Your front-liners must have high trust relationships with their clients. You must experience this first hand to verify customer relations are optimal. It is essential that you are well connected with your top 10 clients and are meeting with them on a regularly scheduled basis. It is common to have a quarterly business review meetings where performance metrics are reviewed and goals/objectives are evaluated. Major customers want to know that you as the manager are tuned into their account.
- **Focus on Big Rocks:** The habit of keeping first thing first is presented in Steven Covey's book; *The 7 Habits of Highly Effective People".*[8] The premise is to prioritize on high leverage activities. High leverage activities can fall into the categories of business opportunities or organizational risk. These need to be acted upon as a priority as they are both important and urgent.
- **Focus on strategy:** As you continue to grow your organization you will naturally rely on many sales and operational strategies that have led you to your current level of success. The challenge all leaders face is discerning what to keep and what to change. All managers are at risk of falling into behavioral patterns that were developed based on past success.

You must embrace "systemic abandonment" of some strategies as your organization grows. An

---

[8] Steven R. Covey, *The 7 Habits of Highly Effective People, (Simon and Schuster, New York, 2004)*

example of systemic abandonment is to abandon a sales territory structure and move to a vertical market structure. Another example would be the implementation of new compensation plans that reward the achievement of strategic objectives. The premise being that the practices and evolution that made the organization successful can only be useful so long. At some point sacred cows must be abandoned for something better.

Remember the expression "when everything is important, nothing is". Determine priorities and take action.

Financial Acumen

Most managers in the low voltage business do not have finance degrees. It has been a fairly common career path for an individual to progress from sales or operational positions into managerial positions. With this career progression the exposure to financial management is generally limited and consequently the individuals financial acumen is weak.

One definition of financial acumen is the keenness and quickness in understanding and dealing with a financial situation in a manner that will likely lead to a positive outcome. Some of the functional skills that will demonstrate your financial acumen include:

- Reading and interpreting profit and loss statements.
- The development of annual financial plans.
- Understanding financial reports, being able to interpret them and knowing how to impact them.
- Understanding how cash flows through the business and how to manage cash flow.
- Understanding how revenue is generated and the legal and ethical guidelines to follow.
- Understanding the application of direct cost and indirect cost and their impact on burden rates.
- Understanding the relationship between bookings, backlog and revenue.

A person with financial acumen is able to evaluate the impact a business decision will have on the financial statements and financial wellbeing of the company.

There is no dispute that to be a successful manager you must have strong financial acumen. And to develop strong financial acumen takes time and immersion into financial reports to understand the business inputs that result in financial outputs.

Suggestions for developing your financial acumen include:

- **Acquire Financial Training:** Obtain basic P&L understanding from on-line videos. Secondarily, financial experts within your organization can train you on specific reports
- **Review your Financial Plan:** Understand what drives the previous year results and the expectations going forward. Seek out insight and assumptions made by the author of the plan.
- **Monthly Review of Financial Reports:** The rhythm of the monthly review of financial reports is essential for progressive learning. Repetition will lead to confidence in your understanding of the data.
- **Teach:** One proven method of learning is to teach others. Consider a month-end training session with your key team members to walk through the financial results and discuss events that had positive or detrimental impacts on performance.
- **Forecast:** Building the next month and next quarter forecast will lead you to think critically about key actions required in order to build backlog, drive revenue, reduce cost or improve cash flow.

For a company to be successful every colleague must understand how the company makes money. When employees are not trained in financial acuity, poor business decisions are made. As the manager you are responsible for understanding the scorecard and communicating results to your team. It is in mandatory to inform your team on the financial performance of the business and work with them to develop action plans to affect positive change.

Section 2 - Build and Execute Strategy

Strategic Planning

As the leader of your organization you are responsible to deliver results. There are innumerable ways and means by which you can achieve results. Many businesses rely on customers discovering them and then responding to their requests. Other businesses have an emphasis on marketing and outside sales effort. The most effective business leaders have come to the conclusion that having a plan (AKA-strategy) is better than not having one.

Mature organizations have adopted the strategic planning process. Senior leadership has embraced the practice and has made the annual planning process a cultural norm. Most leaders believe so strongly in the benefits of strategic planning that they cascade the planning process down through all levels of the organization.

Requiring all levels of management to participate in the strategic planning process is necessary but many managers lack the training and experience. Consequently you must provide the appropriate leadership style to lead your team through the process.

Your enthusiasm is key. Strategic planning requires the manager to think through the plethora of options and decide on finite set of actions. You will need to facilitate and support the team in the creation of the business plan.

In order to facilitate and lead your team through the planning process you need a framework. Let's start with a model.

The Model

There is no absolute model on how to think and plan. There are plenty of books and presentations on the subject of strategic planning. Regardless of the author you will find common elements in every model that will include these actions:

- Confirm that your vision and mission are aligned with strategy.
- Complete assessments of the external and internal environments.
- Confirm your competitive advantage.
- Identify your key objectives.
- Develop work tools that will stratify the benefit versus effort of each strategy.
- Compile a series of strategies that identify the business-building goal and how it will be done.
- Commit to specific actions with either a start date or completion date.

The Process

Regardless of the model that you utilize for building your strategy the ultimate benefit comes from the analysis process. Building an effective strategy takes significant energy on your part as well as all stakeholders who contribute to building the plan.

Many managers find it beneficial to workshop the process. The benefit in this approach is that the leader can assist individuals who struggle with the creative thinking.

Working as a team will tend to stimulate new ideas that may become a key strategy.

Other managers encourage autonomy of their department managers and review their strategic plan for inclusion. This approach may work well for a team that has gelled together over years. A downside to autonomy is that it requires more rework by the manager to ensure sales, operations and service department strategies are completely aligned. Regardless of how "in sync" the management team may be, complete alignment between departments is a nearly impossible when working in silos.

Assessment Tools

Every element related to your business is evolving. Consequently you need to systemically evaluate the various aspects of your business. Doing a deep analysis on an annual basis will open your eyes to potential strategies.

There are many assessment tools to choose from but keep in mind that the assessment tools do not need to be complex. In fact simplicity is preferred. One of the most commonly used assessment tools is the SWOT analysis. This tool uses a 4-quadrant worksheet that identifies the following organizational assessments:

- Internal strengths
- Internal weaknesses
- External opportunities
- External threats

The conclusions you draw from this exercise will guide you potential strategies. You should find that the potential strategies are excessive. If this is not the case you need to think deeper. Your objective is to determine which strategies are your best bets when considering their benefit and their effort to deploy.

	Helpful	Harmful
Internal	**Strengths** **S**	**Weaknesses** **W**
External	**Opportunities** **O**	**Threats** **T**

Business Plan Template

Another important tool is the strategy template itself. Large organizations prefer and often mandate the use of particular templates by all managers. This is logical in that it keeps all leaders within a framework. It also aids the efficiency of senior leaders and executives when trying to understand and assimilate the local strategic plan.

Obviously, if your leadership has provided you with the template you have clear direction of the final product you must deliver. If you are free to create your own plan the template that I recommend is *The One Page Business Plan* from the author Jim Horan.[9]

---

[9] Jim Horan, *The One Page Business Plan, Independently Published, 1998*

The elements included in this template are:

- Your Business Vision Statement
- Your Business Mission Statement
- Your Key Objectives
- Your Key Strategies
- Your Key Action Plans for the next quarter

The fundamental thinking behind this approach is that of "Big Rocks". Focus in on the key elements that will shape or reshape your business. History shows that a thick strategic plan binder looks impressive but rarely will it be opened. A one-page plan can be carried in your pocket or taped to your wall. It has a much better chance of being memorized by you and your team.

Business Plan

Vision	What will my business look like in 3 years?	In 3 years.......
Mission	What is the Mission of the business?	Our Mission is....
Objectives	What are the measurables that determine success?	Metric 1: Metric 2: Metric 3: Metric 4: Metric 5:
Strategies	What is our business building goal & how will we accomplish?	Strategy 1: Strategy 2: Strategy 3: Strategy 4: Strategy 5:
Action Plans	What are my priority actions for the next quarter?	Action 1: Action 2: Action 3:

Benefit to Effort Matrix

Now that you have assessed the current state of your business you have identified numerous potential strategies. Next you must decide which strategies will be your priority focus. The Benefit to Effort Matrix allows you to graphically position each of your strategies on the matrix. This representation will lead you to a conclusion of which strategies should be prioritized into the next four quarters of the year.

Strategies that are ranked as low effort and high benefit would generally be your best bet as a priority. On the other end of the spectrum, strategies ranked as high effort and low benefit would be low priority.

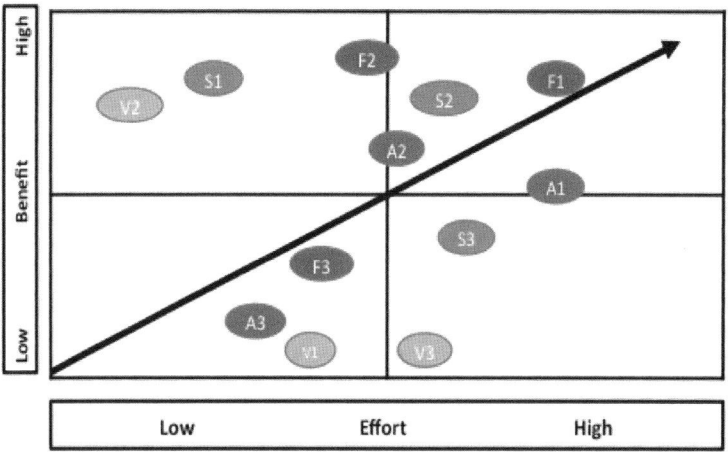

There is much to be gained through collaboration with your department managers and other stakeholders. The interests of all managers must be aligned. Strategic growth goals by sales must be aligned and supported by operations and service.

Strategic planning is not a one size fits all approach. Many managers prefer to create their strategy from an empty slate. Others will build upon the prior years strategy. The key to success starts with the thought process. There is no substitute for your critical thinking.

Sales Strategy

When formulating your strategic plan it is reasonable to start with the sales component of the business. Every business endeavor starts with selling a product or service. A sales strategy logically precedes an operations strategy or service strategy. This premise follows as your organization continues to grow and progress.

In the previous chapter I referred to the elements of your business plan that included:

- Your vision
- Your mission
- Your objectives
- Your strategies
- Your action plans

As the business leader you determine your business vision and mission. Additionally, you determined key objectives for the next fiscal year. Now you need to determine the strategies that will be deployed in order to achieve the objectives.

The process of determining sales strategies should be a collaborative exercise between the sales manager and the sales colleagues. Traditionally, this has been accomplished by providing the sales colleague with a template that they use to develop their sales strategy for the coming year. The individual strategies are then consolidated into an overall sales strategy. The common elements included in the template are:

- **Sales performance:** What was the previous year's performance data? These include bookings volume and margin contribution.
- **Lessons Learned:** What were the highlights and challenges that impacted performance?
- **Key accounts:** Who are the critical accounts for your future success? What is your account development plan?
- **Major projects:** What are the major projects identified for the next fiscal year? What is your capture strategy?
- **Personal development plan:** What are the specific key competencies you are committed to improving? What is the development approach?

The sales colleague is responsible to develop their personal business plan that will detail how they intend to accomplish their objectives. Keep in mind that you and the sales manager will establish the sales colleagues' objectives.

Although it is reasonable and necessary for each sales professional to devise and execute upon their strategy you and the sales manager must provide some guidance and parameters that align with the organizations vision, mission and competitive advantage. One primary consideration is your Go-To-Market approach.

Go-To-Market Approach

The low voltage systems market is enormous; virtually every commercial building uses products or services that your organization can provide. Many considerations go into deciding which markets are best for your organization. Where does your organization have a competitive advantage? Where can your organization add the greatest value for your customers?   Ask yourself the following questions:

- Which vertical markets does your organization have the best operational competency?
- Which product lines does your organization excel in?
- In which markets do you face strongest/weakest competition?
- Are their opportunistic markets as a result of political, social or environmental changes?
- Which markets offer recurring service business?
- Which markets offer greater profitability?

There are countless strategies and approaches that can be successful. Organizational success depends heavily on determining the appropriate Go-To-Market approach.

Most industry participants prefer to sell directly to the end-user of the products and services. The benefit of this approach is that you can emphasize your unique value. It is generally believed that price becomes a secondary consideration in many deals and that end-users (owners) will often pay a premium for perceived quality.

End-user selling requires significant effort in identifying and qualifying opportunities. Finding new customers is a key part of the sales colleague's assignment and requires dedicated blocks of time planned into their week.

The other common market approach is selling through contractors as part of a construction project. This approach can produce equally successful outcomes. Contractor selling is significantly more complicated and requires strong relationships of trust with the industry participants.

One benefit of the construction bid market approach is the low cost of marketing. You don't have to search for customers as the contractors have already identified an on-going stream of opportunities. Value is measured by superior responsiveness, quality, professionalism and integrity. The sweet spot of selling in the construction market is Strategic Project Selling. Not all projects are strategic. A strategic project will generally be large in scope, highly complex and high in dollar value. It aligns with your organization's key competencies and the strategic players with which you have strong relationships. Strategic players include:

- The owner/ end-user
- Construction manager
- Electrical contractor
- Architect and consultants
- Other influencers (fire inspectors, specialty contractors)

Strategic Players

Contractors: To succeed in selling to contractors it is beneficial to "walk in their shoes". Think about the business model of a contractor, whether a general contractor, electrical contractor or a specialty contractor. They are participating in a bid environment, where price often trumps value. Since many of the participants are viewed as <u>equal</u> competitors they are often competing on lowest price. The top tier contractors have financial strength, but the risk of one major project problem, mistake or lawsuit looms large to take them out of business. Being a contractor is not for the weak of heart. What are the goals, problems and needs of a contractor?

- **Goals:** To make a profit, to complete projects on time and on budget, to satisfy client expectations and collect their cash including retainage.
- **Problems:** Managing resources, on-time delivery, effective project leadership, cooperation between trades, managing uncertainty and unknowns, managing risk, talent management and scope creep.
- **Needs:** Strong team members with proven capabilities and positive attitudes, cash flow, partnership and trust.

When you analyze the goals, problems and needs of a contractor and compare those to an end user you will realize that they are different. Consequently, their decision drivers are different. The long-term benefit of the low voltage system is not a concern of the contractor. They are principally responsible to provide a working system that meets a performance criterion with a one-year labor and material warranty. Since the contractor will not be the end-user of the product, they do not value product features, functions and their implied benefits.

Contractors must make a profit. They achieve this through negotiating the best deal from the system suppliers. They can also improve their project profitability through efficiency in field labor. If a supplier has a product that can save the contractor labor units (time), it may benefit the contractor to pay more for that technology. This has been realized with innovative installation methods, smaller conduit requirements, integrated systems, wireless technology and subcontracting various specialty scopes of work.

Contractors meet with countless numbers of suppliers, all of who are trying to pitch their unique value propositions. How do they decide on whom to select? How would you decide? When you have many offers and they all look very similar, lowest price then becomes a key-determining factor. If your strategy is based at winning in the construction bid market your sales strategy must include building high trust relationships with key contractors. This requires consistency in calling on contractor accounts, timely and excellent follow-up, excellent project performance and friendly cooperation. Do this well and over time you will build trust. Contractors will pay a preference for you and your company once you have established yourself as the premier talent. When they face a situation where they cannot pay a preference, they will give you last look to accept the job at the market price.

End-Users: In contrast to contractor selling where the customer (contractor) is much less emotionally attached to the product, end-user selling is heavily slanted in the other direction. For this reason, value will take precedence over price. The value proposition to an end-user is different than that of a contractor. Let's compare:

Value Proposition for Contractor	Value Proposition for End-user
• Competitive price/low price • Product meets all project requirement • Product offers economies in installation • You possess more and better resources • Proven track record of completing similar projects • Knowledgeable in contracting law • Robust safety program • Engineering department support • Project management excellence	• World leader in low voltage/ integrated systems • Mission of service excellence • Proven track record of performance • Best trained specialists to optimize product performance • Customized service offerings to protect your investment • Future-proof products with migration strategies for expansion • Commitment to partnership and continuous improvement through quarterly business reviews • Technologies that maximize system performance

The contractor sale is focused on a singular project endeavor. Your performance on each individual project sets the tone for negotiating future work and shapes an overall perception of your organization. The end-user sale is founded on the objective that parties are entering into a long-term relationship. Granted, if the project is small in scope and price, the view of a long-term commitment may not carry as much weight. On large opportunities the end-user wants to be sure they are partnering with the right organization because the change out of building systems can become extremely costly and challenging. This is particularly relevant to end-users that have an aggressive growth strategy.

The following are the end-user's goals, problems and needs:

- **Goals:** Protect the people and assets of the business, improve safety and security, upgrade obsolete technology, risk mitigation and improve colleague productivity.
- **Problems:** Systems are inoperable, current service provider is not performing to requirements and operational costs are too high.
- **Needs:** Need a trusted partner with high character that is highly competent, technology that will meet today's requirements and adapt well to future needs, peace of mind and confidence in their decision.

Architects and Engineers: Architects and their team of engineers are essential to the construction process of any new building or renovation project. Architects are selected by the owner to lead the design effort. They provide administrative support functions through key stages of the construction process which include:

- Project Inception
- Design development
- Construction documents
- Project administration
- Project acceptance

The architect will also hire a team of specialty engineers to design the structural, mechanical and electrical systems. The knowledge required to design a building and to engineer every aspect of its component parts requires the effort and input from many highly competent individuals.

Low voltage systems are required in commercial buildings. Fire alarms are required based on occupancy type. Sound and communications may include telephony, intercom and paging. Security may include intrusion detection, video monitoring and access control. Mass notification systems, shooter detection, clock systems and data cabling systems are all systems that may be required on a project. Clearly, it is difficult for the most talented sales professional to have competency in all of the features, functions and benefits of these numerous systems. Additionally, It is highly unlikely for an architect or engineer to design these systems without assistance.

As buildings and systems become more complex, architects and engineers need support from industry specialist to educate and guide them on technology solutions that provide the building owner with optimal benefit. The electrical engineer is hired by the architect to develop drawings and specifications. Documents will detail the scope of work and device locations of all electrical systems, including low voltage systems. They are also required to develop a specification manual that details acceptable manufacturers materials, installation means and methods and any other information they deem necessary to communicate project requirements.

Electrical engineers are astute businesspeople who understand they need critical input from industry participants to remain current on product trends and installation materials. They welcome such professionals to educate and train their junior engineers and, in some cases, may even accept the offer to design selective systems.

Listed below are some tactics for your sales colleagues to engage with electrical engineers:

- Request an introductory meeting with the lead engineer to establish relationship and discuss capabilities.
- Offer to conduct a Lunch & Learn for the electrical engineer's team.
- Offer to write the guide specification for the relevant systems on a project.
- Offer to layout and design the systems on a project.

These tactics are not new; in fact they were common for many product providers. Over time product manufacturers have lost momentum in building relationships with electrical consultants. The time is always right for sales professionals to develop a coverage strategy in this area. If you decide to deploy a Go-To Market strategy in the construction market, you would be wise to include a goal to develop relationships with the top electrical engineers in your marketplace.

Many low voltage product manufacturers have marketing positions that take the lead is educating and supporting the consulting community. This approach has been a response to the void left by the sales professionals. The fact remains that the consulting community has unmet needs, and the astute sales professional can capitalize upon this market segment.

Architects and Engineers perform an essential role in the construction community. It is imperative that they perform their work with accuracy and excellence for the contractors to succeed and for the end-user to benefit. Your sales colleagues can provide consultants with vital support that will help them achieve success. By helping architects and engineers succeed your business will be rewarded.

Authorities Having Jurisdiction: The term Authorities Having Jurisdiction, commonly referred to as AHJs is an individual or individuals who interpret and enforce codes and standards. If your organization is selling fire alarm systems and life safety solutions, you are familiar with this terminology referenced in the NFPA codebooks (National Fire Protection Association). State charter defines who acts as the AHJ. There are local fire marshals, county fire marshals and state fire marshals. Additionally, some localities have plan examiners and fire inspectors. All these individuals will be respected as the AHJ when involved.

AHJs do not buy anything from you, yet they are a strategic player that wields incredible power. If you are offering to sell a fire alarm system to a client, regardless of whether it is a new construction project or a renovation project, you will need to submit drawings to the AHJ for approval. The AHJ has a set of published standards that they will adhere to in the review process. This typically includes the NFPA code adopted for a particular year.

It is not uncommon that the AHJ may interpret code sections differently than your team; therefore it is beneficial for your team to establish a harmonious professional relationship with them. Your team offers a significant added value to your client if you can dialogue with the AHJ and gain pre-approval prior to submitting your proposal. I can't overstate the value of having a trusting relationship with the various AHJs. It might not help to sell the project to the owner or contractor, but a poor relationship could cost you severely in project cost overruns if the AHJ becomes difficult.

The following are examples of how the fire marshal can impact project cost:

- Fire inspector determines the fire alarm device spacing is inadequate and requires additional equipment.
- During acceptance testing the Fire inspector walks off the job if minor issues arise (i.e. product warranty) resulting in the need to reschedule stakeholders and lost time.
- Fire inspector will not accept certified pre-test and insists on full retest of the entire system.
- Fire inspector will not accommodate continuous testing through completion, rather allotting small blocks of testing time.

On the flip side, the organization that builds a trusting relationship with the AHJ and creates a partnership with the project stakeholders can avoid most problems and create an excellent experience for all. Building trust with the AHJ takes time and effort. The following are suggestions for your sales colleagues on moving up the trust ladder:

- Request an introduction meeting with the AHJ; learn about their process and pain points.
- Find reasons to discuss code interpretation on a project being developed.
- Offer to conduct a product or code training session to AHJ and associates.
- Submit testing reports to validate project has been certified for AHJ acceptance test.
- Conduct planning meeting with AHJ to review requirements and deliverables.

AHJs are public servants; they serve a necessary role in maintaining public safety. We need each other to help achieve the end-user's goal of building occupancy. Your sales colleagues play an important role as the face of the organization that establishes a level of professionalism and excellence.

Competitive Assessment

Knowledge of the competitive field is a learned competency. It comes from numerous data points that are obtained from client feedback, anecdotal information, business associations, fellow colleagues and industry publications. Knowing your major competitors is important for you in developing your Go-To Market strategy. Additionally, your keen understanding of the strengths and weaknesses of players within those companies will aid you determining whether to use avoidance or confrontational strategies. Once you understand your competition you can effectively develop your major project strategies

It is common to conduct a competitive analysis on an annual basis. Most businesses intuitively see the benefit of analyzing their competition to understand their market strategy. One method used to assess the competition is to utilize the SWOT analysis. This tool uses a 4-quadrant worksheet that identifies the following organizational assessments:

- Internal strengths
- Internal weaknesses
- External opportunities
- External threats

This exercise helps clarify how and where to compete in the marketplace. It will guide decisions on where to invest and focus resources in order to excel over the competition. It also highlights capabilities that need to be leveraged and accentuated.

Most sales colleagues know intuitively which competitors they match up best against. They know their own competitive advantage and think they know that of their competitor. With this knowledge the insightful sales colleague builds a communication plan to shape positive perception of their value proposition. Sales professionals with great communication skills can be the force multiplier for any company.

Major Projects

For a project to be considered a Major Project it must carry a significant benefit to the organization's business. That benefit might be a very large revenue opportunity, a strategic client that might provide national or global expansion opportunities, or it may be the opportunity to execute a complex technology solution. The business is motivated to win these projects, as they are game changers. From a sales perspective, working on major projects can be both challenging and exciting. Major projects require expanded strategic thinking because of their complexity.

Every major project is a unique undertaking. Since major projects are large in scope, owners must create a budget for a capital expenditure. These projects may take many years to complete. The design effort is extensive, and the systems design may progress for over a year. Major projects are a lengthy process, but it is this lead-time that works in your favor if you use such time wisely.

Major projects require the development of a project sales strategy. Templates exist to guide your analysis and planning of your strategy. The key elements of building your sales strategy include:

- **SWOT Analysis:** What are your strengths, weaknesses, opportunities and threats?
- **Project Players:** Who are the decision makers and influencers? What is your relationship with each player (positive, neutral, negative)?
- **Competitive Analysis:** Who is your competition? What are their strengths and vulnerabilities? How do you outperform them?
- **Internal Resources:** Who is on your sales team? What are their responsibilities? Who is the team leader?
- **Key Strategies and Action Plans:** Based on your analysis, what are the key sales activities that will create positive perception of your ability to satisfy the goals, problems and needs of the key stakeholders?

Creating a project strategy takes a concerted effort by the team, but it starts with the leadership of one sales colleague who accepts ownership as team leader.

The responsibility of the team leader includes:

- Communicating the vision and objectives of the project.
- Facilitating and managing activities with the project team.
- Coordinating engagements and communications with the project players.

The blessing of major projects is that you have plenty of time to influence the outcome through a series of sales activities. Most sales activities in the early stages do not take excessive time. These activities are important but not yet urgent. The highly organized sales team can effectively plan sales calls over this extended period that are creative, add value and build positive perception.

Sales Opportunity Summary

Regardless of the Go-To-Market approach or the vertical market focus all sales colleagues must have a roadmap of how they intend to achieve their financial objectives. One tool presented below is humorously referred to as the donut chart because of its graphic presentation. The tool guides the sales colleague to recognize the "Big Rocks", those accounts and projects that will have the greatest impact on achieving their goals.

Many sales colleagues struggle with forecasting how they will accomplish their bookings goal. But history has shown that once guided through the exercise of completing the donut chart colleagues are able to identify 100% of their opportunities necessary to achieve their goals.

Once the sales leader consolidates the sales colleague data into a _team donut chart_ they typically find the top 10 accounts and top 10 projects will result in 100% of the business bookings goal.

This exercise serves to emphasize to importance of "Big Rock" thinking. Also referred to as the 80/20 principle where in 80% of sales booking results will come from 20% of the sales effort.

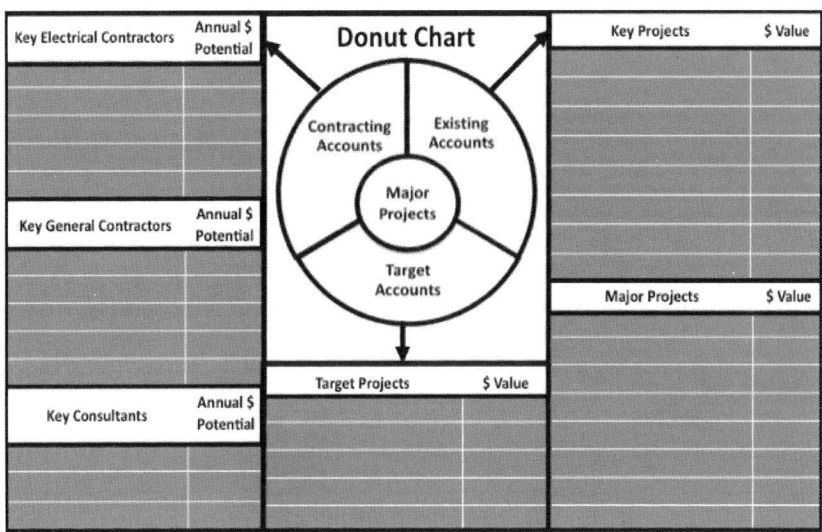

Operations Strategy

It is the responsibility of the operations leader to develop a strategy that aligns with the sales strategy. One could imagine the stress and challenges that would occur if the sales department is booking orders at an ever-increasing volume but the operations department has not prepared themselves for this expectation.

Operations must have a strategy. The operations manager must lead the way in preparing for the future. They prepare for the future by aligning their strategy with the overall business vision and mission.

In the previous chapter I presented a format for the business plan. To be clear, there are many templates and methods for building and presenting a business plan. I do not believe that creativity should be limited for any individual who aspires to create their ultimate utopia. I can attest from experience that whether building a hundred page strategic plan or a one-page business plan the key to success is always based on determining the "Big Rocks" strategy and effectively executing that strategy.

Remember that alignment of strategies is essential. Utilizing the same strategy template between departments is beneficial for consistent thinking by leadership.

For this discussion I will continue to refer to the One-Page Business Plan as the template for building and presenting your strategy.

Business Plan

Vision	What will my business look like in 3 years?	In 3 years.......
Mission	What is the Mission of the business?	Our Mission is....
Objectives	What are the measurables that determine success?	Metric 1: Metric 2: Metric 3: Metric 4: Metric 5:
Strategies	What is our business building goal & how will we accomplish?	Strategy 1: Strategy 2: Strategy 3: Strategy 4: Strategy 5:
Action Plans	What are my priority actions for the next quarter?	Action 1: Action 2: Action 3:

The operations strategy must be cohesive and logical with your vision and mission statements. The objectives are your goals for the next fiscal year. Your strategies answer the question of "What is your business building goal and how will it be accomplished"?

Formation of Your Strategy

Once you have defined your business objectives you need to determine how you will go about accomplishing them. Many managers benefit from having a collaborative brainstorming session with peers and other stakeholders where solutions are shared and ranked.

Operational strategies will typically fit within the categories of colleague development, process management, building capacity and leadership. All of which are interrelated and synergistic.

Let's review each of these categories:

Energize Colleagues: Every achievement of the organization is the result of its colleagues. Logically, to deliver better results the organization's colleagues must get better. Examples of actions that will improve colleague competency, efficiency and commitment include:

- Training and development programs.
- One-on-one coaching sessions.
- Providing colleagues with challenging assignments.
- Building an energized culture.
- Recognizing and rewarding excellence.
- Showing you care about their career aspirations.

Improve Processes: Think about a day in the life of any colleague. What are the processes that are performed with regularity? Every aspect of the business is laden with processes. This is evident when you read the organization's policy and procedures manual where processes are explained in detail.

Why then is quality is still variable? What is the cost of poor quality to the organization?

Business objectives that have a margin improvement metric or customer experience improvement metric will be best achieved through process improvement strategies.

Some considerations for process improvement strategies include:

- Document operational processes.
- Train colleagues on processes.
- Measure processes for quality.
- Improve inconsistent processes.
- Eliminate obsolete processes.

Narrow your focus to specific areas of improvement. For example, if your objective is to improve executed project margins by 2% you might consider the following process improvement options:

- Sales estimating process
- Project review process
- Project turnover process
- Project kick-off meeting process
- Monthly project review process
- Change order process

Intuitively you know which of these processes are robust and which are weak. Select the processes that you believe will have the greatest impact on achieving your objective and build your strategy around it.

Increase Capacity: Assuming the sales department has built a strategy to grow bookings and backlog you will need to build your strategy to increase your operational capacity. Increasing capacity can be influenced by three primary methods:

- Develop the competencies of existing colleagues
- Recruit and hire new talent
- Leverage outside resources

In a growing organization all three methods are necessary. Consider some of the tactical elements:

> **Developing existing colleagues:** Human resource studies have theorized that people learn following the 70/20/10 model. 70% represents on the job learning. 20% represents learning as a result of coaching and mentoring and 10% results from formal classroom learning.

> The challenge with increasing capacity through this method is that it is not timely enough to handle a sudden onslaught of work. The upside is that it is well within your control to initiate the developmental actions that will consistently increase colleague productivity.

> **Adding new colleagues:** Increasing capacity through the addition of new colleagues is a necessity in a growing organization. With the reality that attrition of colleagues can often measure at 10% annually you need to have a strategy for attracting new talent just to maintain output requirements. Add in growth requirements and you've doubled recruiting needs.

> Recruiting and hiring is a major endeavor that can have lasting impact on the business. Hire a top talent colleague and your organization can improve

immediately. The colleague brings unique talents, makes other colleagues better and makes your culture better. Hire the wrong colleague and you will set yourself up for many hours of performance management.

The tactics for recruiting and hiring are well established. It takes persistent effort on your part to develop and execute a plan that attracts industry talent as well green talent.

Recruiting options include:

- Customer referrals
- Professional recruiters
- Job fairs
- College recruiting
- LinkedIn
- Technology hiring platforms
- Internal referrals

As your organization continues to grow, so does your attention to attracting talent. This is a mission critical process.

Leveraging outside resources: The quickest way to react to operational demands is to utilize outside resources. Outside resources are typically identified as one of the following:

- <u>Subcontractors</u> that provide installation services.
- <u>Labor providers</u> that provide manpower to supplement and work side-by-side with your manpower.

- <u>Consultants</u> that provide engineering services or CAD services.
- <u>Intra-company shared resources</u> that provide specialty services.

This method of increasing capacity is generally reactive and far from strategic. But is clearly a potential strategy that could by effectively utilized during peak load periods. Every outsource option relies on building a contractual and business relationship preferably before a crisis hits.

Develop Leadership: The final category for strategy formation is the development of leadership competencies within yourself and your leadership team. The expression "what got us here, won't get us there" is relevant when you think of growing your business and accomplishing your goals. The leadership competencies that got you and your operations team to your current level needs to improve to meet your future challenges.

Your strategy needs to consider the future and what the changing leadership needs will be. Any leadership development strategy should include the following:

- **Assess current competencies:** This will include a review of the leaders strengths and areas in need of development. There are numerous tools available to provide objective assessment information, for example a 360-degree assessment.
- **Build a personal development plan:** The assessment will provide the data necessary to

form a plan. It is beneficial to have a mentor provide input on the top developmental areas. Working this action plan will result in improved key competencies.

- **Coaching and feedback:** Leaders grow and change because they make the decision to. The mentor/coach can play a critical role in facilitating the development process.

Align-Communicate-Execute

Every department's strategy must align with the other departments. This requires sharing, collaboration, brainstorming and commitment to serve the team. Alignment builds synergy and synergy leads to superior results.

The operations strategy needs to be communicated with the entire organization. The strategies do little good if management keeps them to themselves. The strategies are not secrets. Most of your field operations will not retain the strategy without regular reinforcement. Over time more and more of your team will gain appreciation for relevance of the operations strategy. It is up to the leaders to communicate each individual's role in the execution of each strategy.

Lastly, You must ensure the strategy is executed. If you truly believe in your strategy you must overcome all obstacles to see that the necessary time, attention and quality effort are applied to accomplish your strategies. Do this and you will not be disappointed.

Service Strategy

Your service strategy will follow the same approach as described in the operations strategy chapter and will utilize the same templates and models. The key points of the strategy development process includes:

- **Assess your service business:** Utilize a SWOT analysis and other assessment tools to collaborate with key personnel to determine strengths and weaknesses of the service department. Then consider the external environment of opportunities and threats. This information will stimulate initial ideas around strategic initiatives.
- **Review your Vision and Mission statements:** Are you on track to achieving your five-year plan? Is your mission statement still accurate?
- **Define objectives:** What are the objectives of your service business for the next fiscal year?

Objectives

Without knowing any details of your service business I can suggest several likely objectives for your service department. I will rely on you to fill in the metric value.

Here are a few examples of objectives:

- Improve service margins by x%
- Grow service revenue by xx%
- Reduce contract cancellation rate by xx%
- Improve customer satisfaction score by x%
- Improve DSO by x days
- Improve colleague satisfaction score by x%

Formula for Strategy

Remember the formula for strategy is:

The Business Building Activity + How It Will Be Done

Using the first example of improving service margins by x% we begin to brainstorm on the potential business building activities. Here are some potential activities:

- Increase service billable rates
- Increase estimating bid margins
- Improve processes
- Improve efficiency
- Increase price on contract renewals

For each activity there are numerous tactics on how it can or will be done. In the example of increasing service billable rates some tactics on how it will be done might include:

- Communicate the rate increase to all personnel.
- Review existing contracts to ensure annual price increases are acceptable to the customer.
- Develop customer communication plan.
- Update estimating and billing database.

This example would be considered a low effort action with high benefit potential. This should be a priority strategy.

Each objective has its business building activities and means of completion. Once strategies are developed you must prioritize and set reasonable timelines for implementation. Remember that although strategy is important, execution is critical. When you complete your strategy exercise and plot your benefit to effort chart you need to set a schedule for the start and/or completion of each strategy.

Strategy Levers

Identical to the operational strategy chapter, there are primary levers that can and should be considered for achieving most objectives. Although this is not an absolute list, most strategies can conceivably have one of the following business building activities:

- Energize colleagues
- Improve processes
- Increase capacity
- Develop leadership

Key Account Strategy

As your business grows you must evolve. As you acquire more customers and colleagues you must change how you spend your time. Managers often come to the conclusion that a few customers represent a disproportionally large amount of the company's revenue. In my personal experience I have seen my top ten accounts represent 35% of the annual revenue of the business.

Acquiring large accounts is the most efficient path to long-term growth. They provide stability within your business plan with multi-year contracts. The rewards derived from large accounts are offset by the risk of losing these same accounts. To reduce the risk of losing key accounts it is beneficial for you to develop a plan to ensure the long-term retention of these valuable accounts.

Key accounts are the Big Rocks of your business plan. The Big Rocks analogy follows the 80/20 principle in that 80% of the financial results come from 20% of your customers. With this understanding it is clear to see the impact and importance of your key accounts.

Key account management is complex. But the good news is that there is extensive information and training programs that lead the teams to successful outcomes. One such program developed by The Miller Heiman Company is titled the Large Account Management Process (LAMP)[10]. It is suggested reading for teams in search of excellence.

---

[10] Robert B. Miller, Stephen E. Heiman, *The New Successful Large Account Management, (Business Plus, New York, 2005)*

The basic premise of LAMP is this; in order to achieve long-term profitable relationships with your key customers, you must make consistent, measurable contributions to their profitability and their customer relationships. You must make contributions to your key accounts that ensure their success. This is very different than normal sales transactions where parties are focused ideally on a win/win contract for a needed service. With LAMP you are playing the long game with the understanding that by shifting your emphasis to the care and best interests of your client you will be rewarded at the appropriate time.

The first step of the Large Account Management Process (LAMP) is selecting customers that would benefit from your commitment and where the organization can add value to their business operations. Not all customers share a philosophy of partnership. Many customers have a corporate culture where they want to keep a competitive climate between vendors. They prioritize cost management over the value of relationship.

The second step is to assess how your organization is perceived by the account. This is a multi-layered evaluation of your organization as well as the perception of you and each team member that works on the account. Additionally, it considers the perceptions of each stakeholder, decision maker, sponsor and influencer. To assess these considerations the LAMP process requires much analysis by you, sales and operations personnel.

The next step is to build your strategic plan that is qualitative. How will you demonstrate added quality to the benefit of the client? Your goal is to build positive perception within your client's organization and to move up the buy-sell hierarchy. You should be able to determine where you stand with your large accounts. As you build your strategy, you should share your plan with the client. They will guide you to success as it is in their best interest. A client that is unwilling to provide meaningful input may not be a viable candidate for LAMP.

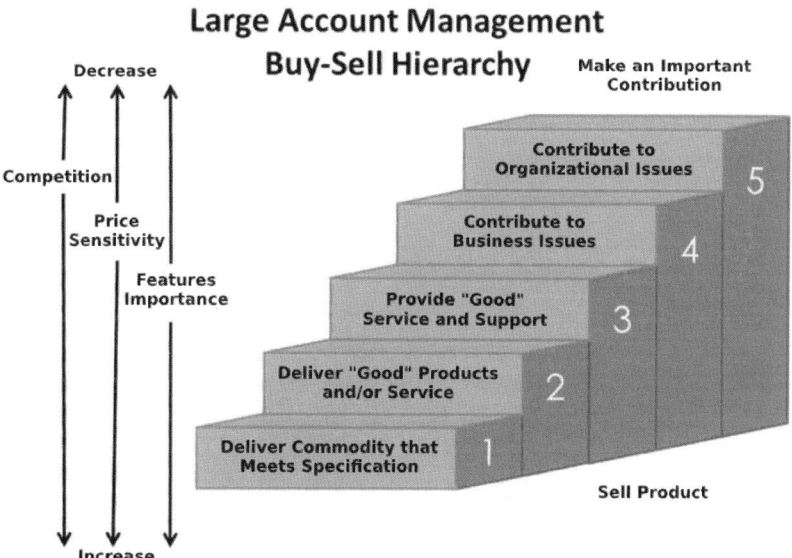

Large Account Management
Buy-Sell Hierarchy

Decrease

Make an Important Contribution

Competition

Price Sensitivity

Features Importance

Contribute to Organizational Issues — 5

Contribute to Business Issues — 4

Provide "Good" Service and Support — 3

Deliver "Good" Products and/or Service — 2

Deliver Commodity that Meets Specification — 1

Sell Product

Increase

Remember the following key points:

- Large Account Management requires significant effort, but the rewards will follow.
- LAMP will require significant mental energy in strategic planning.
- Not all customers are good candidates for LAMP.
- Large Account Management is not a one-person show. It takes a team. You need an account leader. This is generally a senior sales professional.

The LAMP process is one formal program for the strategic management of key accounts. There are others that will share many of the key tenants of strategic selling. Any key account strategy should include the following:

- Assess current state and identify strengths, weaknesses, opportunities and threats. (SWOT)
- Define your vision for the account over the next 5 years.
- State your mission in serving the key account.
- Define account objectives.
- Build account strategies, the business building activities and how they will be done.
- Graph each strategy and tactic on a benefit to effort matrix.
- Prioritize action items. Set the start and or completion date for strategies.

As a final note, it has been recognized that not all managers are comfortable developing business plans or strategies. The same holds true for many account executives. You need to be prepared to provide the appropriate leadership style to your team to accomplish this task. Recall the Situational Leadership model and the matching technique.[11] Provide Direction, Coaching, Support or Delegation as dictated by the colleague's commitment and competency level to the task of building this strategic plan.

---

[11] Ken Blanchard, Margie Blanchard, *Situational Leadership II, 1985*

Alignment-Communication-Execution

Alignment

Results are more achievable when the efforts of many are organized and aligned. The same truth follows when discussing organizational strategies, department strategies and key account strategies.

Achieving alignment of strategies should not be difficult. Managers are fighting the daily battles together. They feel the same pain points. But surprisingly, when an individual creates their business plan and strategy in isolation they can come up with some ideas that deviate quite a bit from the core problems and opportunities. Remember the 80/20 principle, the manager may hit the mark on 80% of the agreed upon points but stray on 20%.

To prevent this from happening you, the leader, must facilitate the strategic planning process. Some of the basic steps in facilitating the process to ensure alignment include:

- Discuss the overarching objectives with all managers and colleagues who will be involved in the strategy planning process.
- Provide a written expectations memo with worksheets that are to be completed prior to the group meeting. Worksheets will include SWOT, One Page Business Plan and Benefit to Effort Matrix.
- Have each manager work with their department personnel to gain insight and communicate the purpose of the process.

- Meet with the management team and brainstorm through the entire process. Ask all managers to state their positions with conviction and challenge issues that don't align.
- As the leader, provide the right balance of facilitation and direction.

It should come as no surprise that these types of alignment meetings bring the team closer together. You and your team have created the one and only Business Plan complete with strategies and action plans. You have an accountability tool. Now you must effectively communicate the plan to your team.

Communication

Now that you have built a comprehensive business plan, you and your management team are fully aligned and committed to executing the plan.

Before you begin executing the plan you need to communicate your strategy to the team. Let's review your objectives:

- **Who do you want to communicate with?** You need to share your business plan with your entire team. Your business plan should not be held as a secret from your team. Every stakeholder plays a role in the achievement of the vision. They might make good contributions even if left in the dark but imagine if they understand and embrace the strategy. How much better could results be?
- **What do you want to communicate?** Share the essence of the business plan. Where is the organization going? How are we going to get there?

Articulate the purpose and meaning of your team's collective efforts. At regular intervals provide progress reports. It is necessary to explain how the execution of strategies or lack of, are reflected in the performance metrics.

- **How do you communicate the plan?** Employ every method available to ensure the necessary information is seeded within each colleague. This is a difficult task. Realizing that not all colleagues understand nor are interested in their role within the strategic plan, you must use your communication skills to ignite interest. Ask and answer the following questions, "What are the needs of my audience?" and "What do I want my audience to think, do, or say after this communication?" With this information you can develop a communication plan that will improve effectiveness and engagement.

- **Why should you communicate the plan to your team?** You cannot achieve your vision on your own. You need a team of energized colleagues. One way to energize colleagues is to explain the importance of their role. Inspire them to perform their role with passion and excellence. Explain what's in it for them when we achieve the mission.

Execution

You have completed the strategic planning process and you have a fully aligned plan with all of your department managers. You have communicated the plan to all colleagues. You feel confident that the plan will result in success for the next fiscal year and beyond.

Unfortunately, you are in for a reality check. The effort of building strategy is the easy part. Execution of the strategy is where the real work begins.

Lets explore why this is. There is little doubt in my mind that managers created the strategies with strong commitment. They had every intention to execute on the plan. The failing comes from the fact that the external world did not get the memo that you needed more time to execute upon the strategy.

The discipline required to change is massive. When you consider all the meetings, calls, communications and activities that you are involved in you must ask, "What can I eliminate from my schedule in order to focus on the strategy and tactics"?

As leader, you must hold yourself and your managers accountable to the strategic plan. The tried and true method to do this is by regular progress review meetings. Invariably, there will be some actions that slip from scheduled start or completion dates. It is up to you to manage these situations with the proper urgency and reasonableness.

The strategies you and your team created are based on your best knowledge and insight. You believe this is your best bet to achieve your objectives. You know you must deliver results. The chasm between your strategy and results is execution. You must push through.

In summary: Vision + Mission + Objectives + Strategy + Action + (Alignment, Communication, Execution) = Success

Section 3 - Build an Energized Team

Success Model

Building a world-class business is no simple task. As your organization expands and grows your challenges expand and grow. Over time complexity finds its way into the organization.

Astute managers develop annual business plans that will deliver desired results. Included in the business plan are strategies and action plans that will accomplish key objectives.

But let's face it, that you can have a great strategy but if you lack the quality and quantity of colleagues necessary to deploy the strategy results will fall below expectations.

With a strong strategy and a strong team of colleagues your probability of achieving success is greatly increased. But achieving organizational greatness takes more than a strong strategy and a talented team. It also requires your team to be energized.

Great managers strive to simplify the complex. In an ever-complex world it is easy for a manager to get stuck in the weeds. It is essential to remember that all outcomes are a result of your colleague's efforts. Organizational greatness is determined by the collective greatness of your colleagues.

The idea of achieving organizational greatness is complex. So is the premise of achieving collective greatness of all of your colleagues. But to simplify this complexity consider a model for achieving success.

Success Model

The success model recognizes three elements of a continuum; energized colleagues, satisfied customers and profitable growth. Thinking through this model you should see that there is a logical starting point on this continuum, it starts with energized colleagues. As indicated on the diagram, the leader's focus is on energized colleagues.

Picture an organization where all colleagues are energized about their personal mission, and the mission of their organization. They understand their role within the bigger picture. They feel respected, valued and loved. They have a belief that they are here to serve the client's needs. They are best prepared to solve the client's business, technical and emotional needs. Your army of energized colleagues is the input that transforms the customer experience into one of satisfaction.

Once the output of customer satisfaction is achieved, the input for profitable growth is possible. The inputs to profitable growth include:

- Timely payment of invoices
- Additional project work

- Service contract work
- Expansion of other low voltage system work
- Favorable references for other clients
- A customer for life

In addition to the benefits that come directly from the customer, another amazing thing happens, your energized colleagues gain higher levels of self-esteem as they recognize the excellence of their work. This builds competence and confidence.

In this last stage, the output of profitable growth now becomes the input for energized colleagues. Because of profitable growth the organization now needs more energized colleagues. The organization now needs to promote from within to expand the culture through mentoring and coaching. The success model continues to expand as the culture of energized colleagues expands.

The leader's focus is on the colleagues. They are the front-liners interacting with customers. They are the ones deploying your strategies. They are empowered to make commitments. They are accountable to deliver results. It is your responsibility to support your team with coaching, direction, facilitation, feedback and recognition.

As the leader, you have numerous ways to energize your colleagues. We will present some means and methods in the following chapters but at the core you must remember that genuine care and concern for the individual is at the heart of organizational greatness.

To achieve your vision of organizational greatness you must have a team of peak performers. Colleagues are not born as peak performers; they develop themselves to become peak performers. You are the architect, the facilitator and the catalyst.

Perception Impacts Performance

The Pygmalion Effect is where an individual's performance is influenced by the expectations of others. In other words, higher expectations lead to higher performance. However, the Pygmalion Effect specifically refers to how our expectations of others affect our behavior towards them. Your awareness of the Pygmalion effect and understanding how it can contribute to colleague excellence is the focus of this chapter.

Many are familiar with the story of the *Man from La Mancha* where the central character, Don Quixote, a mad but kind and chivalrous elderly nobleman, is on his quest to achieve the impossible dream. In one scene he meets a prostitute who he envisions as a fair maiden, Dulcinea. Since Don Quixote sees Dulcinea as a fair maiden and treats her as such she begins to change her self-perception. With her change in her self-image she begins to behave as Don Quixote sees and treats her.

This story is instructive to the power you have within your circle of influence and control. If you believe you have a collection of superstars, your expectations and behaviors toward them will reinforce that belief. Those colleagues will respond to your expectations and behaviors with positivity and confidence. They will be energized and will work diligently to perform up to your expectations.

The inverse is also true. If you believe your team members are substandard and lack key attributes your behavior toward them will evidence these feelings. Your colleagues will "live down" to your beliefs.

How does understanding the Pygmalion Effect help you? You have a significant impact on the people under your care and responsibility. Imagine that each of your colleagues is the most important person in the world because from their perspective, they absolutely are. You must believe in them, you have a team of highly talented professionals. Professionals recognize that they must continue to learn and grow. They look to you for leadership, direction and support to achieve that objective.

Benefiting from the understanding of the Pygmalion Effect starts with you and your self-awareness. Managers who adopt an existing team must assess strengths and areas in need of development. Having development needs does not contradict the Pygmalion effect, each colleague has potential greatness within them, you can help identify their potential and facilitate its development.

How do you apply the Pygmalion Effect principles?

- Genuine belief that each colleague is vital to the team.
- Treat colleagues with dignity and respect.
- Demonstrate that you believe the individual provides a unique skill set that makes the team stronger by their contributions.
- Reinforce your words with consistent behaviors. Be Encouraging and provide the appropriate leadership style to support the colleague.
- Provide genuine public praise for superior performance.

Understanding and applying the Pygmalion Effect does not suggest that you become soft on performance when it is obvious that performance is below standards. What is does mean is that you start with the belief in the individual that they can grow and improve. You provide the tools, support and feedback to facilitate their journey to achieve personal greatness.

When you genuinely believe in each of your individuals and set high yet attainable expectations, they will grow. When they see their growth they will increase their confidence in their competence. This will reinforce your belief and perpetuate the colleague growth cycle.

Energize Colleagues

Motivating others is a key competency for all of the <u>best</u> managers. Managers achieve business objectives through the efforts of others. Logically, managers want to realize the optimal production of their colleagues and their teams.

To realize this utopia you must have a fertile work environment where colleagues are energized. You are best served to create an environment where colleagues are totally motivated to accomplish their mission of serving customers to the best of their abilities.

In reality only a few organizations reach this utopia. Even fewer sustain it. Many authors have researched the ingredients and commonalities of great organizations; two notable studies are *In Search of Excellence* by Tom Peters and *From Good to Great* by Jim Collins. These are both recommended reading. One commonality in both of these books is the critical role of leadership.

Effective leadership has many aspects. One of those aspects is the ability to motivate others. It would be extremely rare for a colleague or team to sustain high performance without outside leadership influence. That influence must be positive, supportive and inspiring. In other words, motivating.

Your goal must be to achieve organizational greatness in the form of profitable growth. Profitable growth is derived from a portfolio of customers who are pleased with your products and services. The pleased customers are a result of your energized team of colleagues. Those colleagues are energized in large part because of your leadership and the culture you are promoting.

Motivating colleagues and teams is not a one size fits all approach. I personally discovered this during my management career with feedback from my managers and direct reports. I found that it was natural and easy to motivate colleagues who were like-minded to me. Additionally, I discovered that my default management style was not motivating for some with life views and attitudes that differed from mine. The key to bridging this gap was to recognize the predominant communication style of the colleague and to communicate in like fashion.

Every colleague is unique and has different motivational triggers. Most people are familiar with Abraham Maslow's hierarchy of needs where human physical and psychological needs must be achieved and sustained in a hierarchical order before progressing to the next level.

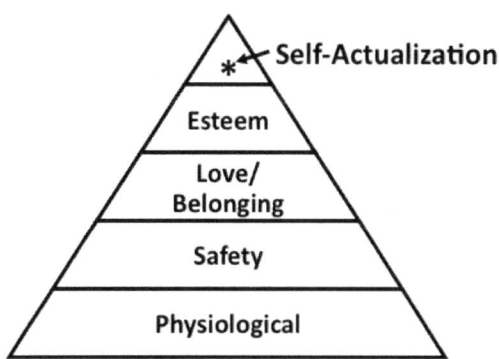

Imagine a colleague that aspires and achieves self-actualization. They have found their purpose and meaning in life and are motivated to maintain that level. Now imagine a team of colleagues who are aspiring and achieving self-actualization in their work. Imagine the energy and momentum such an environment would create.

So where do you start? Focus on the fundamentals:

- Lead with positivity and optimism
- Treat colleagues with respect
- Show you care
- Ask questions and listen
- Communicate expectations
- Give colleagues responsibility
- Hold colleagues accountable
- Set challenging goals
- Provide regular feedback and coaching
- Provide public praise of great performance
- Celebrate success

Beyond these practical suggestions it is important for you to model the way. As leader, the team is looking for you to set the tone for integrity, effort, positivity and courage. Lead and they will follow.

Manage Morale

Early in my career I worked for an international life safety and security company. The local office that I represented had great success for a number of years, the most recent year they were ranked as the top performing security office in the country. Shortly after this award some changes began to occur, several of the top performing sales professionals left the company for new opportunities. The departure of these key team members created a stir within the workforce. The general tone in the office became one of concern. Only a few months earlier the morale was flying high and now the morale was sinking fast.

At the time I was a young sales colleague and I could not appreciate what the General Manager was faced with. Years later I speculated what could have been done to guide morale during that challenging time. The following diagram represents my conclusions.

Achieving Positive Morale

Positive	Neutral	Negative
Add Here	Poised to React to Stronger Force	Subtract Here

The horizontal line represents the entire workforce. The workforce is made up of a number of unique colleagues. On one end of the spectrum there is a group of colleagues who are positive by nature. On the other end of the spectrum there is a group that is negative by nature. In the middle of the spectrum is the largest group that is not positive or negative by nature but is poised to react to the stronger of influences.

As manager, your vision includes building a dynamic prosperous business. To achieve this you must have an energized team of colleagues. In reality, a small percentage of your colleagues operate as your internal leaders and they can pull much of the workforce along to follow their lead. On the other end of the spectrum, there may be personalities who have predominant negative attitudes. Although these colleagues have some valuable talents they may be consciously or subconsciously undermining morale.

With this understanding the objective to maintain positive morale can be achieved in two ways:

- Add more positive colleagues to your team.
- Eliminate negative colleagues from your team.

The objective is to move the middle, the colleagues who are poised to react, to the positive side of the line. You can do this either through addition of positive or subtraction of negative. The net result is positive morale.

Build Culture

Consider the following definition of company culture: "Culture is defined as the values, practices, and beliefs shared by the members of a group. Company culture, therefore, is the shared values, practices and beliefs of the company's employees. While you cannot see or touch a culture, it is present in the actions, behaviors, and approaches of the members of an organization. From hiring practices to how people work, make decisions, resolve differences of opinions, and navigate change, the culture defines the unwritten but very real rules of behavior."[12]

Managers understand the power that culture has in the success of their organization. They can see the evidence that positive culture leads organizations to consistent predictable performance results. With this understanding the astute manager will assess the current culture and determine key areas of focus that will guide culture to a new levels of excellence.

One thing that is certain, culture is not static. Culture is evolving everyday. It is being shaped as you read this sentence. Every thought, words and actions by every colleague is impacting the evolution of your company's culture. These inputs are occurring naturally and generally unconscious to their long-term impact on culture. You however have the power and ability to consciously shape culture through your leadership.

---

[12] F. Jon Reh, *(Understanding a Company's Culture, The Balanced Careers, May 9, 2019)*

Culture does not change overnight or through a management directive. Analogous to improving fitness, consistent exercise with progressive resistance leads to increased strength and endurance. Through your intentional goals and actions you will affect change. Some practical recommendations for shaping culture include:

- **Assess Current State:** What are the values, practices and beliefs of the team? What are the positives that need to be retained? What negatives need to be changed?
- **Communicate Your Vision:** What are you and your organization building? Why is it important?
- **Communicate Your Mission:** Who are the customers we serve and what do we do for them?
- **Connect with the Hearts and Minds of Your Team:** Define the meaning and purpose of what we do. Why are our combined efforts valuable to the world?
- **Define Core Values:** Distill the lengthy list of positive values to the critical few that will establish your core.
- **Build Your Strategic Plan:** With the input from team members Identify key business building activities and the actions steps to accomplish them.
- **Energize Your Environment:** You are the catalyst for cultural change. Your positive energy will spark effort, creativity, initiative and confidence.
- **Communicate:** Be mindful of the needs of your audience. Have a communication strategy that establishes what you want colleagues to think, do or say as a result of the communication.

- **Recognition:** Convey genuine appreciation for the efforts and accomplishments of the team members.
- **Feedback:** Give feedback on a regular basis. Closer to the point of performance is most effective. Negative feedback should be constructive and focused on the behavior not the person.
- **Celebrate Success:** Accomplishing goals and objectives is a natural outcome of positive cultures. Win often and celebrate often.
- **Continuous Improvement:** Leaders set the tone and expectations for the future. They understand that what got us the current level of success will not be sufficient for the future. Everyone must improve.

The recommendations to build a championship culture are unlimited. The expression "It is simple but not easy" is appropriate. Very few of the items listed are complicated, nor difficult. They do require your leadership in the form of analysis, planning, energy, passion, empathy and commitment.

Accountability

Ask yourself this question; what would your organization look like if colleagues did not make and keep commitments? You can envision the frustration and disappointment that customers and coworkers would experience. The thought of an organization that lacks accountability gives all leaders reason for concern.

Accountability is a key principle in building a winning culture. And you need a winning culture to achieve organizational greatness.

Accountability starts with you. You are responsible to deliver organizational results through your efforts and those of your colleagues, suppliers and subcontractors. You create your vision and strategy and communicate it to your team. You monitor and manage the team's progress to goals. You make adjustments over time to ensure the vision is realized.

Holding yourself accountable is the keystone of building a winning culture. But it is not enough. You must hold each colleague, supplier and subcontractor accountable to their responsibilities and outcomes. Each stakeholder should live by the personal leadership mantra of "If it is to be, it is up to me".

Achieving organizational greatness can only be realized and sustained through a winning culture. Build a winning culture is the result of the chemistry of many people, actions/inactions and shared values. Accountability must be one of those shared values.

Acquire Top Talent

Recruiting Colleagues

The goal of improving morale and culture can be impacted most immediately through the addition of top talent. The importance of hiring top talent is obvious yet the recruitment practice of many managers does not reflect a formal process approach, but rather reflects a task that needs to be accomplished.

Successful managers have a clear vision of what they are building over the next five-year period. They have a strategic plan that addresses the business building activities and how those activities will be done. Naturally, as the business achieves its goals and objectives it will need additional colleagues to perform those business-building activities necessary to achieve the vision.

Beyond the addition of new colleagues to achieve growth goals, managers will need to backfill positions for various reasons such as retirements, resignations and termination for cause. In fact it is common to see annual attrition rates of 10% of the colleague base.

Ultimately, recruiting needs to remain a focal point for managers and a key strategy for fast growth organizations. Having stated the obvious, managers have numerous demands that require their time, which often pushes recruiting efforts off of the days priority list. Many managers attempt to solve this problem with the use of industry search firms. Although this approach can provide vetted candidates, it is costly. Additionally, the candidate pools these firms provide are often filled with individuals who are not satisfied with their current employment situation.

All managers have the same desire; to hire the "A Player" in the market place. If that "A Player" currently works for the competition why would they be motivated to leave? Do they have reservations about their current company? Are they looking for career growth at a more stable company? Are they searching for better compensation? The only way to uncover these motives is to meet with prospective candidates and start a conversation.

Consider the following ideas for your recruiting strategy:

- **Define Your Objective:** What positions do you need to hire? By what date do the positions need to be filled?
- **Build Your Plan:** Where do you intend to find candidates? Will you be hiring a search firm? Will you participate in college recruiting programs? Will you be participating in military personnel recruiting programs?
- **Know Your Competition:** Your vision will not be completed in a year. You are playing a long game. Consequently, you should consider the process of recruiting top competitive talent as a courting process. Building trust takes time. Imagine asking a top performer to give up a very comfortable and predictable condition for a potential better life. This courting process takes patience, honesty and evidence.
- **Sell The Dream:** You must be able to sell your vision with conviction and confidence. You are asking candidates to join you on a life-changing journey.
- **Sell The Family:** Recruiting high performing talent has additional challenges. These individuals have

proven track records and often have achieved a level of comfort that their families enjoy. They must evaluate the risk of losing their current comfort over the promise of something better. Meeting with the family and giving them the opportunity to gauge your credibility is a viable strategy.

To achieve organizational greatness you need great colleagues. It all starts with recruiting talent. This does not preclude candidates that come with great attitudes and attributes but lack experience within the industry. These individuals may have the potential for greatness. It would be a great world to have all "A Players" within your organization. That utopia does not exist. The reality is that you may not have the superstar candidate you desire at this time. The business building activity must be accomplished to achieve your vision. You need to hire the best available candidate and then utilize your managerial and leadership skills to support and develop them.

Selecting Colleagues

A wise executive once told a national audience of managers that the best managers were successful with their hiring choices a mere 50% of the time. The essence of the statement is that picking talent is not absolute. As humans we interpret many signals, both verbal and non-verbal. We read into comments and body language. We have many biases that affect our opinions and decisions.

Understanding that selecting the best candidate and hopefully a great colleague is far from absolute. It is in your best interest to become skillful with all aspects of the interview process. Some of the key aspects of the interview process include:

- **Preparation:** A prerequisite of all interviews is having a job description. This assumes that all laws and company policies for posting have been followed. The postings naturally lead to an inflow of resumes' or electronic filings for consideration. As you review the candidate information you naturally need to sort from most qualified to least qualified. To achieve this you need to develop your criteria that aligns with the job description. Not all candidates will come from within the industry so you need to determine "comparables".
- **Interview Questions:** The preparation process requires you to develop a list of questions that will be asked to each candidate.
- **Interview Technique:** One widely accepted interview technique is "situational interviewing". The premise of this technique is that past performance is a strong predictor of future behavior. The list of questions you developed is asked in the framework of telling you a story from the candidates past. In example, Can you tell me of a situation where you were confronted with an ethical dilemma and how you handled the situation? Or, Can you tell me about a situation where the customer was defecting and how you addressed and remediated the relationship? The benefit with this approach is that it avoids theoretical answers and provides greater insight to likely future performance.
- **Scoring:** Part of your preparation process requires the development of a scoring matrix. Your job

requirements and interview questions provide you with the criteria to be scored. Scoring methodology can be a simple 1-5 scale. You may have a weighting for criteria you feel are of greater importance.

- **Individual Versus Panel Interview:** Depending on the situation and culture you may chose to conduct a candidate interview with a panel of cross-functional colleagues. The benefit of this approach is that it will expose biases of the panel. It is not uncommon to have the candidate scoring and rankings vary between panel members. When this occurs it will require discussion and debate to determine why perceptions vary. The downside of panel interviews is that they can be intimidating to the candidate and will clearly have a different dynamic than a one-on-one interview.
- **Interview Environment:** It is good to remember that the candidate is interviewing you and the workplace while you are interviewing them. It is surprising how often managers miss the obvious factors that are shaping the candidates perceptions. A warm reception with recognition that the candidate is expected, a tidy conference room and a professional environment are minimum requirements. Above all the demonstration of your professionalism and business courtesies are critical.
- **Interview Guidelines:** You will be best served if you set clear expectations for the interview. This includes clarifying the time allotted for the interview and notification that you will be using situational interviewing.

- **Stay Focused:** Each interview and candidate poses unique challenges. Distractions can occur while in the interview that can affect perceptions. You may experience a "halo effect" with some candidates where you see attributes that are most pleasing to you or possibly strongly align with your values and beliefs. Beware that the "halo effect" can impact your objectivity.

The interview process will make a lasting impression on the candidates. Your preparedness and professionalism represents a standard of how the organization conducts business and treats people. It is a representation of the culture you are building.

Promote On-Boarding

Over the past decades companies have made a concentrated effort to develop and improve upon on-boarding programs. The need for on boarding is an obvious one, without a roadmap it is difficult to arrive at the destination.

In the context of this book, on boarding is applicable to you, the manager and secondarily to every new colleague hired into your organization.

In earlier days before the term "on-boarding" was in circulation it was common that the new manager was given the keys to the building with a pat on the back and the encouragement of "good luck". With limited direction the manager was expected to figure things out and deliver results. This "sink or swim" approach was viewed as an effective way to separate the wheat from the chaff. Over time organizations became more enlightened and realized that providing orientation, direction and training were in the best interest of the organization and manager.

The following excerpt is from the Greatness Guide - a Coaching Manual for Sales Professionals in the Low Voltage Industry. The chapter on On-Boarding is relevant for you and your personal development. Additionally, it is the message that you and your leadership must promote to every new colleague you hire.

Companies have recognized the need and benefit of having formal on-boarding programs for new colleagues. It is intuitive that business models become increasingly complex as the business matures and grows. Consequently, it is in the best interest of the colleague and the company to monitor and control the dissemination of knowledge to simplify the complexity.

The on-boarding program for sales colleagues is customized. It is designed to increase your knowledge of organizational processes, tools and resources to aid you in becoming effective and efficient in your assignment. The program provides a guide for the activities that are to be completed within the first 30, 60 and 90 days respectively. The intention of the on-boarding program is to guide and support the training process to its completion and in alignment with the 90-day review and subsequent goal setting.

Successful on boarding is dependent upon you. The personal leadership mantra "If it is to be, it is up to me" applies to your realization of on boarding program benefits. History shows that new colleagues want to begin contributing quickly and prove they are adding value. This is natural and welcome. Additionally, it is understood that new colleagues can quickly become overwhelmed with work assignments that will appear to take priority over their on-boarding responsibilities. You are accountable to stay the course and achieve milestones as set forth.

Understanding that you will realize meaningful benefit from the on-boarding program in direct proportion to your personal investment, I encourage that you bring genuine enthusiasm, active listening and feedback to this critical process. The content of the on-boarding program is massive and therefore much of the information can be forgotten if not applied soon after learning. To support absorption, you are strongly encouraged to provide a weekly written summary of your progress and lessons learned. Additionally, research has found that learners have demonstrated a 90% retention rate when they teach others their new knowledge within 3 days[13]. I encourage you to apply both strategies with excellence.

Napoleon Hill stated, "A person cannot exceed mediocrity without the help of others." [14] With this on-boarding program you will have the assistance of your manager, peers and several subject matter experts (i.e. functional leaders in human resources, national accounts, operations etc.). These individuals will support you along your journey. While they are committed to facilitating key parts of your on-boarding experience, they are all carrying full workloads. You can honor their efforts by coming prepared and energized to scheduled meetings and calls.

Although this excerpt refers to sales colleagues, the message is applicable to all new hire positions as well as yourself.

One might imagine that having an on-boarding map would naturally lead people to the planned destination. This is often true, but analogous to life, many people abandon or ignore maps for their personal reasons. You play a central role in shaping the culture of your organization. Communicating the importance of the on-boarding program is essential. Holding colleagues accountable to their on-boarding maps is aligned with building a culture of excellence.

---

[13] National Training Laboratories, Bethel, Maine

[14] Napoleon Hill, *The Law of Success, pp. xxi (The Penguin Group, New York, 1928*

Provide Coaching and Feedback

As a manager you are pulled in many directions. You are often required to handle reactive events. If you allow this as a common practice, you will find that your entire day will be consumed by the priorities and needs of others. Not surprisingly, many individuals stop trying to plan their activities because they have subordinated their "Big Rocks" to the demands of others.

We have already established the importance of planning in your quest for organizational success. Central to your priorities and planning is the communication of your vision, mission and strategy. One of the essential mediums of accomplishing this is through meetings.

Planned meetings are a proactive activity. But just because they are planned does not make them effective. To achieve effectiveness first requires you to define your objectives. What do you want your audience to think, do or say at the end of your meeting? While developing your agenda you must consider the emotional and intellectual needs of your audience.

Coaching meetings can be an effective communication tool. Their purpose is to build trust, motivate, and develop colleagues. A key question is; can you succeed without conducting them? Certainly many managers do not embrace the practice of coaching meetings and may have a level of success. On the other hand, elite leaders intuitively understand the power of coaching meetings.

Some considerations on coaching meetings:

- **Frequency:** The frequency on your coaching meetings will be dependent on the number of direct reports you are managing and other priorities that may be pressing at the current time. Weekly one-on-ones are recommended in the early stages of building your team. As relationships develop the interval may be extended.
- **Format:** The format is limited only by your creativity. The manager will generally take the lead in creating and driving the agenda. This is natural in that the colleague is not familiar with your thinking and will not know your objectives and vision until you educate them. Once you develop a rhythm with the colleague it is beneficial to share the responsibility of agenda development and meeting collaboration.
- **Agenda:** The agenda should consider the needs of the individual and the needs of the business. Understanding that these two considerations can lead to extensive discussion topics, it is up to you to determine a manageable agenda. As previously stated, the topics need to focus on developing the colleague, building confidence and trust.
- **Culture:** Shaping culture starts with you. Building a culture that clearly demonstrates colleague development is a priority. It stands to reason that continuous improvement of each colleague will lead to improved organizational performance. Coaching meetings are a best practice. When the practice of coaching meetings are cascaded down through the organization and performed effectively,

transformation will occur. Be cautioned that your subordinate managers may not be enlightened or competent in conducting coaching meetings with their direct reports. In these cases the coaching meetings will not have the desired effect. You will need to inspect what you expect and provide the appropriate coaching and feedback.

In his book *The 7 Habits of Highly Effective People*, Steve Covey discusses beginning with the end in mind.[15] Your vision is the end state. The coaching meeting is an important tool that will facilitate organizational growth and the achievement of your vision.

Performance Feedback

Achieving your goals, objectives and vision will be accomplished through the talent and effort of others. When you consider the impact of talent and effort on your outcomes you can logically see a model:

- Poor talent and poor effort will result in poor results.
- Average talent and average effort will result in average results.
- Excellent talent and intense effort will result in superior results.

There are obviously degrees to each of these scenarios but I to achieve your vision you need a team that possesses excellent talent and applies intense effort, a Super Team.

---

[15] Steven R. Covey, *The 7 Habits of Highly Effective People, pp. 102-153 (Simon & Schuster, New York, 2004)*

Building a Super Team must be your key objective. There are many strategies that you will employ to achieve this. One of those strategies will be developing your colleagues. Human resource studies theorize that people learn from three primary means; on the job experiences, coaching/mentoring and formal training. Each of these learning avenues will involve some form of leadership or supervision to support the colleague's development.

Although each colleague is accountable for their own development, leaders see the development of their colleagues as a mutual benefit. Consequently, they are engaged in the oversight and progress. One of your key responsibilities is to provide feedback to colleagues on their performance.

Feedback can be both formal and informal. An example of informal feedback is cited by Spencer Johnson in his book, *The One Minute Manager*, where he explains the practice of one minute goal setting, one minute praises and one minute reprimands.[16] The key take-away from these practices is to provide timely feedback to the performance event.

Here are some considerations on performance feedback:

- **Provide Timely Feedback:** Feedback is most valuable when it is provided close to the event. As time goes by, memories become less exact to both parties.
- **Soft on People, Hard on Performance:** Feedback should always focus on behaviors. The value of the person must be held sacred. You must set high

---

[16] Ken Blanchard, Spencer Johnson, *(The One-Minute Manager, 1982, Publisher William Morrow)*

standards of performance and be able to separate the person from the behavior.

- **Build Trust:** Colleagues are more inclined to accept feedback if you have established a high level of trust with them. Trust is measured in terms of both your character and competence.
- **One-on-One Meetings:** One-on-one meetings provide an excellent forum to give performance feedback. Colleagues and managers establish a rhythm and trust which makes for productive discussions and agreements.
- **Document Timely:** The power of your feedback is enhanced when it is documented timely. This is true for both positive and negative feedback.
- **Annual Performance Reviews:** Many managers and colleagues dislike the annual performance review process. For many colleagues it appears to be the first time their mistakes are highlighted. Objective managers realize they could do a better job of addressing and documenting negative performance throughout the year. To make annual reviews productive consider using the 5/1 principle. The 5/1 principle asserts that humans are most receptive with a ratio of 5 positive comments to one negative comment. If you find that negatives far outweigh positives you may realize that you have not been providing feedback throughout the year or that you have neglected handling a more severe performance issue.
- **Public Praise and Private Reprimand:** These two practices are powerful to building positive culture.

Genuine appreciation and specific acknowledgement of notable accomplishments build the individuals esteem and reinforce behaviors. Private reprimands show respect for the colleague's dignity. Conversely, public reprimands can have a negative impact on culture and diminish your status as leader.

Your constructive feedback and effective coaching with colleagues will accelerate development, build culture and move you closer to your vision.

Section 4 - Manage and Improve Processes

Planning Process

Business Planning

Do you believe that a well-developed business plan is essential to achieve organizational success? It would seem logical that every professional manager would embrace this practice but history shows that far too many managers and supervisors do not.

Why would managers not embrace the practice of business planning? Some managers don't know where to begin the process so they never get started. Others get stalled by the complexity of infinite possibilities and become confused. Others may find that they do fine by reacting to short-term opportunities, consequently the urgency to develop their long-term plan does not present itself.

Industry leaders embrace business planning. The specifics of how business plans are developed vary from person to person. They are often a reflection of personal preference and creativity. Organizations will often provide business-planning templates to align thinking between operations.

The template is not the plan. The plan is your comprehension of your current reality, clarifying your goals and deciding your priority actions. These thoughts are then documented in order to further assimilate, challenge and share

One of the planning tools I have endorsed is *The One Page Business Plan* by Jim Horan. As the author notes, the One

Page Business Plan is a framework for continuously moving your business to the next level of discipline.[17]

The framework of the business plan includes the following:

- Vision
- Mission
- Assessments
- Objectives
- Strategies
- Action Plans

Vision: What are you building? The first step is to develop your vision statement. An effective vision statement is concise and will answer these questions:

- What type of business is this?
- What markets does it serve?
- What is the geographic scope?
- Who are the target customers?
- What are the key products and services?
- How big will the company be, and when?

Mission: Why does this company exist? The second piece of your business plan is to define or refine your mission statement. This is where your passion is expressed to the world. Good mission statements are motivating to colleagues and customers. An effective mission statement will answer these questions:

- Why does this business exist?
- What are we committed to providing to our customers?

---

[17] Jim Horan, *The One Page Business Plan, Independently Published 1998*

- What promises are we making to our clients?
- What needs, desires or problems do our products and services solve?
- What is our unique selling proposition?

Assessments: Before building a solution you need to diagnose your current state. Assessments are an essential activity that will highlight strengths and weaknesses in each element of your business. The common tool used to accomplish this is the SWOT analysis. (Strength, Weakness, Opportunity and Threat)

SWOT Analysis	
Strength	**Weakness**
Opportunity	**Threat**

The SWOT exercise is a visual tool that will aid you throughout your business planning process. The observations and insights gained from this exercise will be used in the formation of strategies and action plans.

Objectives: What business results will be measured? If working for a regional or national organization it is likely that you're objectives are established for you. If they are not, it is prudent to consider objectives around bookings, revenue, profitability, cash, and process management. All objectives must be specific and measurable.

Strategies: How will this business be built? Strategies are the roadmap to how you will build your business. The strategies you may develop are limitless, but from a practical standpoint some strategies will have a far greater impact than others. Don't boil the ocean. Key in on your best strategies and remain focused and diligent.

Strategies		
Strategy	Business Building Activity	How It Will Be Done
1		
2		
3		
4		
5		

Action Plans: Once your strategies have been determined the next step is to prioritize your actions. Some of your strategies will be complex that have numerous action steps. Other strategies may be quick hitters. Determine which action plans will be deployed each quarter. Be reminded that you will always be faced with unplanned urgencies so be reasonable on the number of action plans you set forth each quarter.

For most organizations the business planning process is an annual rhythm. But the exercise does not start from scratch. Rather, it is a continuum. The annual process requires you to reflect on the past years accomplishments and failings to determine why some strategies and action plans succeeded while others did not. These are critical inputs as you build subsequent business plans.

Financial Planning

Every business must develop a financial plan. Financial plans may also be referred to as your budget. The financial planning process for mature organizations is very formal. Even before the current fiscal year is completed, planning for the next year must commence.

The financial planning process is very analytical. It requires the efforts of you, your management team and your sales team to see the future and make logical predictions based on business trends, customer demands, internal capabilities and best guess scenarios of how the business will grow.

The process of building your financial plan starts with comparing your previous years budget to your year-to-date performance. This comparison will evidence which of your previous assumptions were correct and which were flawed. This information becomes essential as you carry some assumptions forward while modifying others.

Financial planning requires you to think about cause and effect of various investments. A common example is the addition of personnel. When adding personnel, whether sales, managerial or support there is the expectation of increased revenue. The timing of the expense will always precede the revenue benefit. In a growing organization the logic is to add personnel early so they may ramp up and become productive. The effect of these actions will likely result in higher costs without offsetting revenue for a lag period. The duration of the lag period is one of many assumptions you must make.

Some of the key inputs required in building your financial plan include:

- **Year-Ending Backlog:** You will need to determine the amount of additional bookings for the remainder of this year less work that will be executed and pulled from your backlog.
- **Bookings:** You will need to determine the month-to-month bookings for the next fiscal year.
- **Backlog:** New bookings will increase monthly backlog. A healthy business has an ever-increasing backlog.
- **Contracting Revenue:** As your backlog grows so should your monthly contracting revenue. An important metric is your turn-rate ratio. This is the percentage of backlog that is converted into revenue each month. Knowing this average provides a useful check on your projections.
- **Contracting Margin %:** This is an important guidance metric for your sales team. Your current year will provide you with recent history, which

will stimulate analysis of your business trending that may need to be altered.

- **Contracting Variance:** Establishing accurate burden rates and managing field productivity are essential in maintaining a favorable variance. Current trends will provide guidance on budgeting and necessary strategies to improve.
- **Service Revenue:** If your business has multi-year service agreements you can count on maintaining a portion of your service base year-to-year. Billable service work should rarely retract year-to-year and should be expected to grow naturally over time. If you have dedicated service sales colleagues, revenue growth should be aligned with sales bookings expectations.
- **Service Margin %:** As a general rule service margin % should be higher than contracting margin %. Service margin % should be expected to improve through various actions such as rate increases, improved efficiency and bundling of services.
- **Selling Cost:** Current trends provide a starting point. What is the expected number of new hires for the next fiscal year and what month will they be added?
- **General and Administrative Cost:** Current trends provide a starting point. What are the expected new hires for the next fiscal year and what month will they be added? What recurring expenses are expected to increase next-year? What capital investments planned?

The outcome of your efforts will lead you to re-examine your assumptions. Your profitability projections may not meet your growth requirements. The important consideration is that growth is a must. The process will require you to predict the future with a balance of optimism and pessimism.

Recovery Plan

In a perfect business world you will develop your financial plan with careful consideration of all trends, opportunities and risks. You will break your plan down into monthly periods and then execute the plan. Results will follow your plan and all goals will be achieved. The reality is that this never happens. There is variability because complex business cannot be predicted with accuracy.

One challenge in building your plan is that you are expecting to achieve growth based on expanding the existing capabilities of your organization. This expansion is based on increasing the productivity of colleagues and adding more colleagues. This is a logical assumption. The significant challenge is predicting when the benefit of expanded capabilities will bear fruit.

In example, You expect a developing sales professional to be able to produce 10% more the following year as they build their sales pipeline, build client relations, learn about upcoming opportunities and become more efficient in work processes. All these assumptions are logical but not necessarily linear.

Another example is your expectation to hire an additional sales professional the following year that will contribute towards your bookings performance goal. Hiring talent requires the time to complete many activities such as:

- Soliciting and interviewing candidates
- Conducting background checks
- Performing on-boarding tasks
- Building a sales plan
- Performing sales call activities
- Building sales pipeline and closing work

The lead-time before realizing consistent sales contribution is many months. All this time you will be paying for an expense without offsetting financial benefit.

The key point is that the financial plan you built cannot predict the absolute timing of performance events. Some events are far more beneficial and positive than were expected. Other events are negative or even disastrous. For this reason you must continually:

- Assess your business performance.
- Learn about your colleagues and their capabilities.
- Improve processes that impact efficiency and productivity.
- Develop a winning culture that is committed to delivering results.
- Assess external influences; key customers, existing project risks, competitive risks and major projects.

This assessment process is something you will do continuously. Naturally you are constantly evaluating reality, building perceptions and taking action on situations. But the formality of adjusting your plan is more deliberate. Month by month you gain insight on your business and marketplace. You make some quick adjustments early in the year to stay on course. Sometimes the adjustments do not work and the financial plan compared to actual results becomes a major concern. At this point you are in need of developing a recovery plan.

A recovery plan requires you and your team to evaluate the financial plan and look at the performance gaps. Can you capitalize upon areas that are over-performing to make up for shortfalls? In areas of under performance determine corrective action plans to narrow the performance gap.

Recovery plans start with a brainstorming session with your team. They follow the same structure as your P&L statement and will capture specific opportunities and actions that will boost performance in order to achieve the committed results. The key is identifying specific opportunities and actions that can be assigned to individuals who will deliver financial results.

Some of the considerations when building your recovery plan:

- **Bookings:** Which new bookings can be turned into revenue this fiscal year?
- **Backlog:** Which projects in backlog can be completed this fiscal year? Can we accelerate any projects? Will client accept and pay for materials this fiscal year if work will be performed next fiscal year?
- **Work in Progress:** Which projects have an opportunity for savings? Which projects have risk? Which projects have change orders which have not yet been booked?
- **Contracting Revenue:** What are the top 10 revenue drivers for remainder of the year?
- **Service Revenue:** What is your backlog of service calls and plan to complete? What are the top 10

service revenue drivers for the remainder of the year?

- **Contracting Variance:** Is the burden rate set correctly for full absorption of costs? Is downtime being managed to target levels? Should burden factors be adjusted?
- **Contracting Margins:** Are sales bidding margins optimized to market conditions? Are sales estimates accurate as compared to job performance?
- **Service Margins:** Are service billable rates adequate? Are service processes and scheduling optimizing the efficiency and talent of field personnel?
- **Expense Management:** What discretionary spending can be deferred until next year? Can open job positions be deferred until next year?
- **Sales Expenses:** What sales expenses can be curtailed? Can open positions be deferred for hiring until the end of the year?
- **Cash:** What are the top 10 collection opportunities? Which customers may be willing to pay early?

Recovery plans work because they are focused and invoke urgency and accountability. If they work then why don't we operate under these parameters all the time? Believe me when I say that it has been tried, but discovered that there is a necessary rhythm to the business. That rhythm is as follows:

- Develop your Financial Plan and Strategy.
- Assess of your colleagues and processes daily.
- Conduct monthly business review.
- Create business forecast for next 30 and 90 days.

- Conduct quarterly review of sales and department managers business plan.
- Develop recovery plan and manage its execution.
- Achieve your goals and objectives.
- Repeat

Performance Management Process

Monthly Management Review

Once the financial plan is approved you are off and running. Analogous to running a race you need to check your split times to determine if you are on pace to achieve your goal. The split time checks in your business are conducted each fiscal month.

In a perfect world you would build your business and financial plans and results would follow as anticipated. This is seldom the case. In your business there will always be surprises, both good and bad. The bad surprises need to be analyzed with the goal of overcoming and preventing their occurrence in coming months. On the other hand, good surprises should lead you to examine how you might duplicate or leverage opportunities.

The monthly performance review is primarily focused on financial performance. The review consists of comparing actual performance to your current months forecast. Additionally, you will be comparing how the performance lines up with your financial plan.

The monthly results are the bi-product of the cumulative efforts of your colleagues. To recall and synthesize how those efforts translated into results takes considerable input from your management team.

Here are some recommendations for making your monthly review meeting effective:

- **Prepare:** Once financial reports are available, conduct your personal review and look for deviations from forecast. Make notes of variances and their likely causes. Have each of your managers conduct a similar evaluation of their department.

- **Schedule:** As soon as reasonable, schedule a meeting with your team to review the financial reports in a formal setting.
- **Agenda:** The objective of the meeting is to analyze the past and to adjust for the future.
- **Attitude:** It is important that meetings remain balanced. When the financial performance results miss the mark there will naturally be concern and emotion. Remain constructive. Other months will overachieve and be cause for enthusiasm.
- **Human Errors:** When reviewing financial reports there is always the possibility of recording errors and omissions. Revenue recognition in financial systems occurs when costs are posted to projects or when service orders are invoiced. Pushing the wrong buttons or failing to process transactions can inaccurately reflects true performance. Catching these mistakes requires a deep dive into reports. Once mistakes are found the correction may be made through journal entries by the financial management department.
- **Action Plan:** The result of the monthly performance review meeting is a list of action items that each manager must focus on.
- **Report up:** Every manager has a boss. The boss is seeing the same financial reports as you and will be looking for insights on factors affecting the results, positive or negative. Be timely to provide an executive summary. If results are significantly below

forecast you will want to have an action plan prepared to discuss.

- **Continuous Improvement:** You and your team should strive for continuous improvement in every aspect of your business. The monthly performance review meeting is a process that must continually improve. The monthly rhythm, when done right, will increase insight of the intricacies of the business. This insight will lead you and your management team to be more proactive in process controls.

There are several additional benefits derived from the monthly performance review process. These include:

- **Financial Acumen Training:** Many managers struggle with understanding the financials. It takes many repetitions for a non-financial manager to gain competency here. The monthly rhythm provides a forum to test understanding and increase competency.
- **Process Improvement:** The monthly review meetings have a way of exposing recurring problems. This recognition should lead to action plans to improve weak processes.
- **Defines Priorities:** The insight gained from the review meetings will highlight actions and projects that will demand your time and attention.
- **Leads to Strategic Thinking:** The monthly performance review will lead you to a greater awareness of the cause and effect of your decisions. In other words what should we do more of and what should we do less of.

You must understand your business. The monthly performance review process will help you achieve this. With greater understanding of your business comes your responsibility to take action.

Executive Reviews

Executive reviews are commonplace for regional, national and international companies. It is an efficient process for busy executives to gain insights on their business units. Executives rely on local leaders to inform them on the state of the business and provide them an appropriate level of detail.

The executive will ultimately determine the appropriate level of detail, but generally you can expect them to provide an agenda and possibly a template for presentation. Understandably, the executive is better able to process information and compare and contrast strategies and best practices when uniform presentation templates are used.

Executive business reviews serve several important functions that include:

- **Financial Performance Review:** Executives have the financial results and have reviewed them in advance of your meeting. They will be looking for you to explain the story behind the numbers. In areas where results are <u>better than plan</u> be prepared to highlight the reasons for success. In areas where results are <u>behind plan</u> provide some background as well as your corrective action plan.
- **Strategy Review:** During your financial review you will touch on many points of your business strategy. Your presentation should weave a story

that details your strategy and relate how the strategy has impacted the financial results. The elements of your strategy should include discussion on your vision, mission, objectives, key focus areas and action plans. It is easy to get into the weeds with too much detail so be mindful of your audience.

- **Colleague Review:** All results are a bi-product of your team members. You will be presenting on the performance of individuals as well as groups. You must be objective while you paint the best possible picture of your talent. Executives want to know about your top performers and the reasons for their success. Additionally, they want to know about average and under-performers and your plan to manage them to higher levels of performance.

- **Positive Perception:** During your time with executives they will be building perceptions about many things. They will be forming opinions on your competencies, your commitment, your professionalism and your leadership. Your preparation, energy and command of the day will go far in building trust and confidence.

- **Team Development:** Executive presentations will generally include your local management team. The department managers will be expected to present on their business unit. Many department managers are intimidated and nervous to present to executives. It is incumbent upon you to ensure your team is prepared and has rehearsed for the day.

- **You are the Owner:** The key takeaway for the executive must be that you are a composed, competent and confident leader. You have a plan and are executing the plan. You are building a culture that will achieve organizational greatness.

Executive business reviews are high stakes. They are an opportunity for you and your team to shine. Do not miss the opportunity to set the standard of excellence.

Risk Management Process

Project Risk Review

Your sales team is responsible to find opportunities that align with your strategy. The sales colleagues will identify many opportunities that look promising from their vantage point. In reality, not every sales colleague can be objective when they look at opportunities. In fact many opportunities have greater risk than reward, which are not understood by the sales colleagues. With this understanding you need to have a formal process and guidelines to manage risk.

The objective of the project review process is to assess risk, review cost estimates and to determine if the opportunity aligns with organizational capabilities and resources. The effectiveness of the project review will be determined by the commitment and competency of the colleagues involved.

Here are some recommendations for your project review process:

- **Define Expectations:** It is up to you to establish expectations for your sales and operations personnel. Articulate the objective of the project risk review process. Communicate how your expectations align with your vision, mission and strategy.
- **Written Guidelines and Procedures:** Giving a pep talk will provide a short burst of compliance, but will not create a lasting habit. Written guidelines will reinforce your verbal expectations. The guidelines will include the roles and responsibilities

of the various stakeholders. It includes the timing of when the review needs to occur with respect to the proposal due date. Guidelines will also define review thresholds based on financial parameters.

- **Standard Forms:** A key premises of process control is to remove variability. Mandating the use of standard forms is a best practice to remove variability. Standard checklists and data collection forms are extremely beneficial in creating a culture of discipline and consistency. Consistency leads to competency, competency leads to confidence and confidence will lead to improved results.
- **The Sales Colleague Leads:** The sales colleague is responsible to present the opportunity to you and other stakeholders. The logical flow of the meeting should include an overview of the opportunity, the scope of work, the checklist of inclusions and exclusions, project risks with mitigation strategies and review of cost estimate.
- **Risk Review:** All participants must be objective of all potential risks and then to determine mitigation strategies. The team must determine the value to be included in the cost estimate for the various project risks identified.
- **Collaboration:** It is essential that sales, operations and management collaborate and come to agreement with the project's merit and cost estimate. Operations must embrace the project once it has been sold. Sales must be thorough and transparent in the review process.

The effectiveness of the project review process relies on your leadership. You set the expectations. You provide the direction, coaching and feedback to your team. Your consistent reinforcement will improve risk management and operational excellence.

Work in Progress (WIP)

The term "Work in Progress" refers to all of your open construction contracts. The process of reviewing all of your open projects is of critical importance in running your business.

There are many logical reasons why you must have a systemic review of all open projects but the absolute requirement is based on United States tax law. The common business model for low voltage companies is to perform construction contracts and to perform service work. United States Tax law provides for two revenue recognition systems as follows:

- **Long-Term Contracts:** These refer to projects that are completed over a longer period of time and will often bridge multiple fiscal years. Tax law requires that revenue be accounted for in the year that costs have been incurred. This is a serious issue. Due to the accounting abuses of major corporations, laws were enacted to invoke penalties for accounting manipulations. The Sarbanes-Oxley Act of 2002 was created to require publically held corporations to define and abide by internal financial controls and to attest to their accuracy. Revenue is generated as cost is applied to the contract, not through invoicing

- **Short-Term Contracts:** The vast majority of service projects fit into this category. This includes service calls ranging from one day to several weeks as well as over the counter parts sales. Revenue is generated through invoicing.

Although the Sarbanes-Oxley Act is required for publically held corporations, the process is logical and recommended for privately held companies as well.

Central to your WIPs process is first to define your process and then to abide by it. Some of the considerations for your WIPs process include:

- **Leadership:** You or your operations manager is responsible to lead this meeting.
- **Timing:** WIPs meetings need to occur monthly. Most managers find the third fiscal week of the month to be the appropriate time.
- **Attendees:** Key personnel include your operations manager and the project manager. Depending on the size of your office you may chose to have additional participants but keep in mind that more people can mean more distraction from the agenda. If you have numerous project managers it is preferred to have them scheduled for separate meetings.
- **Format:** Every project should be reviewed in chronological order. The questions that are asked to and answered by the project manager include:
  - Are the costs to date accurate? Are all costs posted correctly?
  - What are the costs to complete? Do we need to re-estimate additional costs? Do we have the potential for savings?
  - Is the project completion date accurate?

- **Preparation:** The project manager should have complete knowledge of each project's status prior to attending the meeting.

Although it is not recommended that the WIPs meeting become a problem solving or strategy meeting, they often migrate in that direction. The downside of this behavior is that the meetings can become excessively long. The upside benefit to you is that you gain deep insight into projects which allows you to evaluate risks and opportunities. You also learn much about the skills, knowledge, strengths and weaknesses of your project managers.

The WIPs meeting is an essential process in managing your business. It is a monthly rhythm that provides great insight. Great insight will aid you in decision quality.

Quality Management Process

To achieve organizational greatness you must deliver results. Delivering high quality products and services at the right time are paramount to customers. Delivering top line growth and profitability are paramount to the organization. A quality management process will help you achieve both objectives.

The objective of the quality management process is to improve the quality of products or services your company provides. Quality can be defined as high accuracy, compliance with applicable standards, and high customer satisfaction. The objective of the quality management process is to measure key aspects and achieve improvements.

High Accuracy: Accuracy is about hitting the target. The closer you are to the bulls-eye the greater the accuracy. To be able to measure accuracy you must define the target. Each position within your organization performs activities that are essential to the overall business process. In fact the business process is the compilation of numerous processes. The key to quality management is to define processes, educate and train colleagues on the process and then to measure accuracy.

A common industry term is "Key Performance Indicators" (KPIs). Senior leaders define the KPIs for the businesses in order to measure progress in the areas they feel are most important to achieve organizational objectives. By creating scorecards they can compare and contrast business units, which essentially measure output results. The output results are a reflection of quality and process. At the local business unit you must mimic this approach and determine the critical metrics you will focus on that will have the greatest impact on success. Remember that inputs (activities and processes) lead to outputs (results). You must determine the optimal number and the most relevant inputs and outputs to measure. Remember the 80/20 principle.

Compliance with Applicable Standards: The low voltage industry has many standards that have been institutionalized by local, state or national authorities having jurisdiction. Examples include the National Electrical Code, Underwriters Laboratories and National Fire Protection Association. Additionally, Cities, Counties and States create their own requirements for building construction and improvements. In regards to quality management processes you must structure, educate and train your organization to comply with the applicable standards.

Construction projects present another set of standards. Architects, engineers and contractors have their own set of rules and requirements that must be performed to. This includes such activities as safety compliance, daily reports, submittals, drawings, payment requests, bonding, insurance, testing and certification reports.

Quality issues revolving around compliance can have a detrimental effect on customer satisfaction. Impacts may include loss of goodwill, loss of future business or delay in cash payments.

High Customer Satisfaction: Ultimately each customer decides if you are providing quality products and services. How do you measure performance in this area? Most companies utilize a customer survey process to aggregate results and track performance on a macro level. The benefits of customer surveys are limited due to the fact that customers have become overwhelmed and cynical by the constant request of feedback on their performance.

Companies who are succeeding and growing face the risk of losing intimacy with their customers. As you gain <u>more</u> clients you have <u>less</u> time to dedicate to each client. You will be challenged to develop process solutions that will address this problem.

There are several key strategies that organizations use to build high customer satisfaction:

- **Provide Value:** How does the price compare to the quality of the product or service? How does your customer compare your price and value to your competitors?
- **Build a Culture of Customer Care:** Reinforce vision, mission and strategy to your team on a consistent basis.
- **Passionate Colleagues:** Hire, train and retain colleagues who possess empathy and believe in servant leadership.
- **Processes:** Adopt best practices and ensure compliance.
- **Continuous Improvement:** The expression "What got you here, won't get your there" applies to customer perception. The world expects more and

will reward those who innovate and provide better value.

- **Show You Care:** Passionate colleagues will follow a passionate leader. You lead the way in building culture and demonstrating servant leadership. By showing you care about clients your team will be inclined to follow your lead.

Quality management is a never-ending process. You start where you are today and you build a plan to get you to a better state. What you focus on will certainly show results. There are many tools and techniques that can be deployed to improve processes, including programs such as Total Quality Management (TQM), Six Sigma and kaizen events. Within these programs are effective discovery tools, which are geared to improve efficiency and accuracy.

Change Management Process

Change is necessary to achieve organizational greatness. Our day-to-day lives see numerous incremental changes that do not take much energy or effort to accept. On the other extreme we experience transformational changes. These types of changes can offer challenges to all organizations.

To achieve your vision your organization must grow. Growth will require change. It is up to you to lead change by communicating why the change is necessary and how this change will align with your vision.

One widely accepted change management model was developed by Jeffery M. Hiatt referred to as the ADKAR model. [18]The five-step model is as follows:

- **Awareness** of the need to change
- **Desire** to support and engage in change
- **Knowledge** of how to change
- **Ability** to execute change
- **Reinforcement** to sustain change

Awareness: Leaders continually assess the current state and desired state of the business. You as the leader will need to prepare your team for change. This will require you to communicate a compelling reason to change from the current state to a new state.

Desire: Group behavior will follow a bell curve that will include innovators, early adopters, early majority, late

---

[18] The Proski ADKAR Model

majority and laggards. Look to your innovators and early adopters as internal leaders that will support your initiative. **Knowledge:** Leaders educate their team on how to change from the current process to the new process. What is the timeline? What are the new systems or procedures? Who will they go to for support when questions or challenges arise?

Ability: Once the team has been given the knowledge they will need to develop competency on the new process. They will have new tools to become proficient with.

Reinforcement: Team members will need feedback early and often to support the change process. You have a responsibility to keep the team informed on progress through both metrics and anecdotal success stories.

Not all colleagues will embrace change. You must be prepared to address this likelihood with laggards. This may require some direct non-negotiable mandates.

Change management is a process. All processes must continually improve. The change management process has many variables. You need to control the variables by having an effective communication plan and execution plan.

Leading Change

The discussion of organizational development implies change. The word "development" means to improve, to make better, bigger or faster. In order to improve your organization, you must make it better, bigger or more efficient, you must develop it. You must make changes.

Making changes is easier said than done. Many colleagues are resistant to change. The reasons for resistance are varied; they include fear of the unknown, complacency, ego, and other priorities.

When it comes to transforming your organization you cannot avoid the reality that change is a constant. In fact change is occurring daily within your organization. Some of the change is intentional but often change is casually occurring as colleagues learn and adapt within their environments.

Not all change is good. Without the proper knowledge, insight and vision many changes may be detrimental and inefficient. To minimize this possibility managers must lead change. They must understand the dynamics of both group and individual change.

Leading change is a process. Ken Blanchard developed a model for leading change that he describes as Situational Leadership. Blanchard explains that change leadership is not a one size fits all approach. Rather leaders must match their leadership style to the colleague's commitment level and competency level to the task they are attempting to perform.

Development Level	Leadership Style
Development Level-D1 • High Commitment • Low Competence	**Leadership Style-S1 Directing** • High Directive Behavior • Low Supportive Behavior
Development Level-D2 • High Commitment • Growing Competence	**Leadership Style-S2 Coaching** • High Directive Behavior • High Supportive Behavior
Development Level-D3 • Variable Commitment • High Competence	**Leadership Style-S3 Supporting** • Low Directive Behavior • High Supportive Behavior
Development Level-D4 • High Commitment • High Competence	**Leadership Style-S4 Delegating** • Low Directive Behavior • Low Supportive Behavior

This matching process requires you and the colleague to be in agreement on their development level to the task at hand and then for you to apply the leadership style that matches.

From personal experience I can attest to the powerful impact this approach has on colleague development. At first it is not intuitive. It takes effort and practice on your part but with each attempt your competency will improve. Increased competency will lead to increased confidence and your confidence will inspire and earn the trust of your colleagues.

This chapter provides a highlight of Situational Leadership. I recommend that you gain an in depth understanding and examples through books and videos available on this leadership model.

Section 5 - Increase Organizational Capacity

Organization and Structure

To achieve organizational greatness your current organization will need to evolve into something bigger, better and different. Your organization must transform.

Transforming your organization is complex, challenging and very fun. Consider how organizations adapt and evolve. Everyday your colleagues are learning about their environment. Colleagues solve problems and learn from each experience. Work processes are improved out of practicality. Colleagues improve efficiency and effectiveness.

Much of organizational learning happens naturally. There are many variables that impact organizational development and transformation. Consider some of the factors affecting organizational transformation:

- **Leadership:** The most important ingredient in transforming an organization is you, the leader. You are the catalyst that sparks excitement within the hearts of your colleagues. You communicate meaning and purpose to your team. You set the standard.
- **Shared Vision:** As leader, you must clarify what you are building. You are receiving input from up and down the organization but ultimately you must live and breathe the vision as your own. Secondly, you must share your vision with the entire team. Your intention is to make your vision a shared vision. Getting the entire team to advocate your vision is a lofty goal but you need a critical mass to believe the

vision is worthy of their efforts and passion. Relate and connect with your team and answer the question "What's in it for me?"

- **Culture:** Culture will either support or reject your transformation efforts. A positive culture that has a shared vision, believes in personal leadership and embraces change will certainly have superior results over the inverse.

- **Strategy:** Although some transformation is happening serendipitously, planned transformation happens with strategy. Strategy aligns with vision and mission. Define the business building activities and how they will be done. Involve your team.

- **Communication and Reinforcement:** Your colleagues are deluged with day-to-day activities. Most colleagues do not live in a strategic mode. Regular communication and reinforcement on progress to goals is essential.

- **Milestone Success:** To achieve your vision you and the organization must keep pace by achieving interim goals. Key goals include revenue growth, profitability growth and free cash flow. Additionally, milestones that indicate progress in colleague engagement, development and satisfaction are paramount in building enthusiasm. Enthusiasm is essential in the transformation process.

One additional thought on transformation is on the premise of <u>systemic abandonment</u>. The premise surmises that at various points in the life of an organization the organization must abandon some of the processes, beliefs or sacred cows that were central to their success. This is a very challenging concept and not intuitive. Recall some situations in your past where technological, economical, political, societal or environmental conditions forced change and transformation upon you. The advice is to lead change. When you lead change you have more control of outcomes than when change is invoked upon you.

Your vision is to achieve organizational greatness. Transformation is necessary. Lead change.

Developmental Model

In 1965 Psychologist Bruce Tuckman came up with the developmental model of "Forming, Storming, Norming and Performing". In his paper titled *"Developmental Sequence in Small Groups"*[19] he describes the path that teams follow on their way to high performance.

Can you recall how these four stages were manifest in your past? When you consider this model does it not also reflect the stages that every new colleague entering this business must go through?

Understanding this model is useful in your quest to transform your organization. You will recognize this developmental sequence every time you hire a new colleague, make a structural change or make a process improvement change.

The developmental sequence parallels the Situational Leadership model. Consider this linkage between the two models for both individual development and team development:

---

[19] Bruce Tuckman, *(1965) Development Sequence in Small Groups, Psychological Bulletin*

- **Forming:** When embarking on a new endeavor individuals and teams are deferring to the leader to lead the way. To guide them and provide tools, training and resources necessary to succeed. The leader provides _**direction**_. In the forming stage there is usually a high level of enthusiasm and uncertainty by the individual and team. As leader, you must harness this energy to build momentum as you head into the storming stage.

- **Storming:** As the individual or team begins to execute upon the plan there will be errors, roadblocks, confusion and frustration. You must keep in close contact with the colleagues during this stage and solicit continuous feedback. Your leadership style at this stage is _**coaching**_. You need to provide clarity, facilitate problem solving and offer encouragement. Presuming you have given the team the training, tools and resources to accomplish the objective they now need the repetitions and practice to move into the norming stage.

- **Norming:** In this stage we see individuals and teams consistently performing the tasks and delivering expected results. They understand their duties and objectives. Things are going as planned for the most part but occasionally a crisis may occur. During this stage you generally provide a _**supportive**_ style of leadership. You support the individual or team through encouragement or constructive feedback. They no longer need direction for the majority of issues. They need the confidence of their leader.

- **Performing:** The final stage of the developmental sequence is high or peak performance. During this stage the individual or team displays a high level of commitment and a high level of competence. At this stage the appropriate leadership style is one of _**delegation.**_ Your colleagues have the autonomy to perform their assignments with minimal supervision. You are able to reap the timesaving benefits that come with high performing colleagues. You focus on encouragement and facilitating the requests of the team.

The development sequence model is logical. So is the situational leadership model. The key is to understand the development stage that your colleagues are in. Teach your organization about the developmental sequence. Raise their awareness of how development happens. As team-members understand how the human development model and the situational leadership model work together they will be empowered to learn and grow.

Structure

You may remember an automobile commercial with the tag line "form follows function". That tag line conforms to the topic of organizational structure in that structure follows function.

In the context of developing your organization, the design of your structure is a starting point. It is the essence of organizing the organization (pun intended).

Structure is best explained though graphical representation with a structure chart. It is commonly depicted with a hierarchical diagram with senior leadership on top then cascading down to show each level of supervision then each direct report. When complete, the graphic captures every colleague in the organization.

This process of developing your structure chart helps you in several ways:

- **Clarify Accountability:** The structure chart will make clear where each colleague fits into the reporting structure and who their supervisor is.
- **Identify areas of Matrix Management:** It is common to have shared resources between managers such as administrators, project managers, technicians and installers. The structure chart will force the thought process of who is ultimately responsible for the management and development of those colleagues.
- **Facilitate Brainstorming:** Building your structure will generate ideas on how to best support growth of your organization. Besides the functional and matrix structure you may have considerations for remote geography management and small team management. Another brainstorming exercise is to draw what the organization of the future will look like in five years. Begin to imagine who your future leaders are and where they fit into the structure.
- **Visualize Growth:** Periodic review of your structure will aid you in determining resources needed in the future. Generally, incremental colleagues are needed to produce ever-increasing output results in sales and operations. At certain junctures added supervision is required to support the organization.
- **Assess Organization Development:** Structure charts are an effective means to communicate the

strength and development level of your organization. A color-coding method of green, yellow and red provides viewers with a simple interpretation of organizational risk and maturity. In this exercise "green" indicates competent performer, "yellow" indicates developing colleague and "red" indicates an underperformer.

The structure of the low voltage industry has been defined and streamlined over many years. To remain both competitive and profitable you must understand the best in class productivity metrics and align your structure closely with those metrics.

Additionally, you must take a hard look when considering the addition of support personnel. More people are not the solution to many of your challenges. Stay lean and always look for productivity improvements.

Some organizations have implemented virtual structures where leadership is remote. In other words, eliminating the resident manager. This model tends to look appealing from a cost perspective. From a practical perspective local leadership is essential for long-term success.

Roles and Goals

Your structure chart will graphically represent all the positions within the organization. Each position should have a formal job description that is used when recruiting candidates. These job descriptions provide the essential details on the roles, goals and impact the position has within the organization.

At the time of hire, colleagues understand their role within the organization. As time progresses, the role of the colleague can morph and change. As the organization grows junior positions evolve into senior positions. Senior positions must take on the role of mentor or team lead. Additionally, selective colleagues may be asked to take on assignments outside of the original job scope to support organizational needs.

All colleagues need to understand the various roles within the organization. To best serve their clients they need to understand who does what and how the various roles work together to deliver fluid and flawless service. Analogous to a playbook, you need to understand your assignment as well as the assignments of your teammates.

Transformation of your organization is the result of achieving many goals. In your role as manager, you must facilitate, challenge, align and monitor the goal setting and goal accomplishment within your organization.

Goals can be described in several tiers:

- **Individual Goals:** Each colleague must create annual goals. This will address performance goals, professional development goals and customer goals. Goals should follow the SMART model. These goals are initially created by the colleague and then reviewed, approved or modified by the colleagues' supervisor.
- **Department goals:** Each department manager must establish team goals for their business unit. These will be a combination of financial performance goals and activity goals. This resembles a matrix of input goals and output goals. For example, a service department may have an input goal to accomplish product training with an output goal to improve first-call-fix-rate. Another example would be for a

sales colleague to attend LAMP training with the output goal to increase sales production within key accounts.

- **Business goals:** The objective of the business is the accomplishment of the key financial goals of revenue growth, profitability and free cash flow.

Some practical advice when it comes to goals:

- Goals should be aligned throughout the organization. When individual goals, department goals and business goals align and support each other the probability of organizational success is increased.
- Select a manageable number of goals. Be mindful and strategic in determining goals. Big impactful goals should have an absolute focus. More goals are not always better and in some cases are de-motivating.
- Goals need to be reviewed regularly to ensure progress is being made. This is especially true for professional developmental goals. Many colleagues set training or certification goals and will delay or forget about them until the year-end. This typically results in failure. Institute regular goal progress reviews into your one-on-one meeting agenda.

Defined roles and goals are essential to transforming your organization. Understanding every colleague's role and then establishing and accomplishing relevant goals will build competence, confidence and momentum toward your vision.

Business Rhythm

A consistent business rhythm will increase the effectiveness of you and your team. There are multiple ways to increase your effectiveness outside of working harder or longer. One way is to develop routines and habits.

Positive habits are a reflection of discipline and personal power. Once an individual associates routines and habits with their success they will embed them into their thinking and make them a cornerstone to their management approach.

The following are some thoughts and considerations around business rhythm:

Daily habits: What are the activities you embrace that maintain or expand your energy, intelligence, passion, spirituality and attitude? What is your routine for planning the day, week and month? Do you prefer to do your planning early in the morning versus end of day? The habit of planning is a necessary discipline.

Weekly rhythm: Much of your time is spent on managing information and communicating. Take for instance weekly sales meetings. Sales meetings are essentially the sharing of information between manager and colleagues. It also includes communicating expectations, requirements, strategies and knowledge. Your weekly rhythm is like gravity for your team. The weekly cycle is the ideal time frame to develop group norms and expectations.

Common weekly meetings include:

- Sales meetings
- Construction operations meeting
- Service operations meeting
- Managers meeting
- Cash collections meeting
- Safety meeting
- One-on-one meetings with direct reports

All of these meetings are intended to be a continuum. There is no end date but rather an on-going development of the business through the development of the individuals and the synergies created by the combined efforts of those individuals.

Monthly rhythm: There are twelve months in the fiscal year. Those twelve months are analogous to a twelve game football schedule. The primary objective is to win the games, to get into the playoffs and win the championship. In your business your primary objective is to win through the achievement of your goals and objectives each month.

When you build your monthly rhythm you should consider the likely demands by week.

Week one will require time to close out the prior month. Review financial reports, analyze the results and build response plans. Planning for the month is advisable in week one.

Week two and three are essential for executing the plan and strategies. Scheduling external meetings with key clients, business partners and other stakeholders are a priority. Additionally, scheduling time with field colleagues to gain insight on project performance and challenges.

Week four will shift your focus to closing out the month in order to deliver forecasted financial results. Many of the activities involve administrative efforts to ensure resources are scheduled to complete commitments that generate revenue. This also requires communicating with your team members the priorities in order to win the month.

Quarterly rhythm: The quarters of the fiscal year become an ideal time to compare and analyze progress-to-date against your business plan. At the onset of each year, sales colleagues and managers will have developed their business plan. It is ideal to have these plans reviewed and adjusted as necessary on a quarterly basis.

Annual rhythm: Financial and business plans are built each year. Each department manager and sales colleague must develop their plans that support the overarching plan.

Annual performance reviews are a necessary routine in your business rhythm. As each fiscal year ends it is important to reflect on past performance for the business and the performance of each individual contributor.

The business rhythm describes activities of what to do and when to do them. But the activities themselves do not guarantee superior results. Some additional considerations to maximize the effectiveness of your business rhythm include:

- **Energy:** Leaders know the power that enthusiasm and positivity brings to culture.
- **Agenda:** Much of the business rhythm involves meetings. If those engagements lack intentionality or purpose they can become an energy suck. It is up to you to drive purpose and meaning.

- **Respect Time:** Start meetings on time. Finish meetings on time. Time is a finite resource. Your behavior will define its value.

Over time your business rhythm must evolve. With success and growth your focus will shift. Remember the quote, "What got you here won't get you there". Experiment and embrace change.

Team Development

Talent Management

Talent management is a term used to describe all aspects of a colleague's journey within the organization. When considering the life cycle of a colleague it can be detailed in the following stages:

- Recruitment
- Development
- Performance
- Promotion
- Retention

The big picture of talent management is that all results from your business are the direct output of all your team members. As basic as this statement is, the logical extension is that the better the talent, the better the results. How can you improve the talent of your organization? Let's refer to the stages of talent management.

Recruitment: One sure way to improve business results is to hire top talent. This may include a proven performer from within the industry or from a related field. These colleagues can have an immediate impact. In reality, these colleagues are often the most difficult to obtain since they are already successful and have all the perks and accolades that are provided to top performers. The other end of the spectrum is the recruitment of new talent into the industry. This includes college recruiting, trade school recruiting or raw energy individuals. As your organization grows you will need a mix of both veterans and rookies.

Recruitment is the first stage of the talent management process. Arguably, it is the most important stage. Hiring the right colleague will have a lasting impact. Hiring the wrong colleague will be a drain on your energy and organizational resources.

Development: You hire colleagues to perform to a certain level of expectations. But to ensure colleagues perform to expectations you would be wise to facilitate their development. One of the first developmental tools to be utilized is the on-boarding process. Your goal should always be to maximize the talents of your team. Ultimately, you want to help colleagues realize their full potential. You do this through creating an environment and culture where colleagues are energized.

Performance: The better the collective whole of individuals perform the better the organization performs. To achieve your vision of superior performance you are responsible to manage the performance of team members. The term "performance improvement" has developed a negative connotation because it generally applies to colleagues who are not performing to expectations. But consider that the entire theme of talent management is to facilitate performance improvement. The leader guides the life cycle of every colleague to achieving personal greatness. You play a valuable role as coach for your colleagues providing them with valuable feedback and direction. One of the proven managerial approaches is the application of Situational Leadership.

Promotion: Humans want and need to grow. Stagnation can have negative impacts both at the individual level as well as the organizational level. Growth creates excitement. When individuals realize personal growth their confidence and self-esteem grows. When the organization is achieving its goals and objectives opportunities become abundant. As the tour organization grows, new positions become available. The opportunity for the promotion of prepared colleagues presents itself. Promotions are a key component of your talent management strategy. As your culture self-identifies as an organization ripe with growth and career opportunities colleague attrition will be a reduced risk.

Retention: Colleague turnover is inevitable. It is also costly. In the low voltage industry it is common to see colleague turnover of 10% and greater. Consider the implications of constantly having to recruit, on-board and train 10% of your colleague base. Additionally, consider the new positions required as a result of business success. It's easy to understand the efforts required on your part that will result from these new hires. Now think about the benefits realized if colleague retention is improved through greater effectiveness in recruiting, development, performance and promotion processes.

Talent management is a key strategy to achieving your vision. When executed effectively you will energize colleagues, build momentum and shape culture.

Training and Development

The expression "What got us here, won't get us there" directly relates to the topic of training and development. To realize your vision you and your entire team must get better, you must adopt the practice of continuous improvement.

There are several ways you can improve your organization, the first is to hire excellence. Hire colleagues who bring skills, knowledge and attitude that are superior to your current team. The second means is to improve efficiencies through process improvements. The third means is to improve competencies through training and development.

Training and development can be viewed as an input/output relationship. Training is the input activity of instructing colleagues on new knowledge and concepts. This includes the knowledge of products and skills. Additionally, training is the practice of applying this new knowledge thereby transforming it into improved competencies.

Organizational development is the output from training and learning. Human resource experts have asserted that there is a formula for colleague development referred to as the 70/20/10 model. 70% of development comes from on-the-job experience. 20% comes from mentoring and coaching while 10% comes from formal training. With this understanding you see the greatest impact in your colleagues' development happening every day in the trenches.

Since on the job experience is the "big rock" in colleague development it stands to reason that managers should focus on influencing the developmental process. There are several ways you can facilitate development:

- **Leadership Style:** In his book, Situational Leadership II,[20] Ken Blanchard describes the matching of the appropriate leadership style to the colleagues' development level associated to the specific task. When a colleague understands the level of direction and support they can expect from their learning

---

[20] Ken Blanchard, Margie Blanchard, *Situational Leadership II, 1985*

becomes efficient. Once colleagues are trained on the Situational Leadership model they understand the process of personal development.

- **Goal Setting:** Setting SMART goals are ideal for establishing expectations. Goals need to be realistic and attainable. Achieving goals on a regular basis builds positivity and confidence.
- **One-on-One Coaching:** Regular one-on-one meetings are the ideal forums to discuss development. Intentional conversations about colleague progress will enhance and accelerate development.

The second learning dimension is mentoring and coaching. Most colleagues do not have a formal mentor assigned to them; rather, colleagues observe veteran colleagues and adopt their practices. But this does not mean that you should not embark on a formal mentoring strategy for developing colleagues. The best mentoring results come when both the mentor and mentee are excited about the opportunity to share and learn together.

The third learning dimension is formal training. In many respects this is the easiest learning dimension to deploy because it is typically an event with a specific and measurable outcome, conducted in a controlled environment within a defined time parameter. Think about vendor product training or on-line certification courses.

Assess the developmental needs of both your organization and your colleagues. Develop your growth plan and share it with your team. Align your plan with your vision and remember that organizational development should be intentional rather than accidental.

Continuous Improvement is a natural process:

- **Diagnose Your Organization's Developmental Needs:** Work with your department managers to establish priorities.
- **Create Your Organization's Developmental Plan:** Select 2 or 3 focal areas per department at a time. Do not attempt to boil the ocean!
- **Execute the Plan:** Remain disciplined and tenacious.
- **Track Progress:** Record the specific areas in which the organization has gained new knowledge or skills.
- **Repeat the Process.**

Training Plans

Think about a professional football team. At the beginning of each season the players are invited to training camp. The overarching purpose is to prepare for the season ahead.

Training camp intends to improve the physical condition of players, work on positional skills, learn the playbook and develop synergy with teammates through drills and scrimmage. The accomplishment of these objectives cannot be left to chance by ad hoc decisions on a daily basis. Rational thinkers can see that a detailed plan is critical to manage the development of both players and coaches.

If all teams in the NFL follow a similar practice for developing and preparing their teams we can conclude that it has been proven as a best practice. Training plans are used because they work.

Is it important for you to have a training plan for your team? If the obvious answer is "yes" then why do so few managers have one? The intention of this section is to present key considerations that will aid you in the creation and deployment of your training plans.

What is the Scope of a Training Plan? : The term "continuous improvement" is self-explanatory. In order for you to achieve your vision your team members must improve. This applies to every colleague. As manager, you must diagnose the developmental needs of your team members. As in our NFL example, a team has a training plan that has a hierarchy of needs. First the organization considers overall team needs. Secondly, they consider offensive/defensive/special teams needs. Then positional needs and individual needs. In your organization the scope may include the following:

- **Entire Team:** Compliance training, ethics training, safety training.
- **Management Team:** leadership training, financial training, strategic plan training.
- **Sales Team:** Product training, selling skills training, Strategic sales training, account management training.
- **Service Team:** Product training, customer skills training, software and programming training, troubleshooting training.
- **Construction Team:** Code and standards training, materials and methods training, project management training.
- **Administration:** Business systems training, project coordination training.

How do you Create a Training Plan? : As your organization grows, so does the complexity of your training plan. Engage your management team in the creation of your master plan. Start with your vision and identify your organizational priorities. Conducting a SWOT analysis will point you in the right direction. Additionally, annual colleague performance reviews provide insight on the development needs of each colleague. Brainstorm with your management team and develop an annual training matrix.

Accountability Versus Facilitation: As the leader of your organization you are accountable for creating the master training plan. You should solicit input from your management team but you own the final product. Once the plan is created you play an essential role as facilitator. You have a vested interest in communicating the importance and desired outcome of training investments. But the accountability of learning falls to the colleague.

How People Learn: As previously presented, the 70/20/10 learning model is recognized as a reasonable belief on how colleagues learn. Managers tend to focus on the formal training when building their training plans. There is nothing wrong with this approach. But consider how organizational learning is occurring the other 90% of the time. How can you leverage job experience and mentoring/coaching to be an intentional element of the training plan? Here are a few ideas to consider:

- **On-Boarding New Colleagues:** This is an essential part of the training plan for new hires. A positive on-boarding experience propels colleagues forward by providing them with essential information that supports efficiency and effectiveness.
- **One-on-One Meetings:** One-on-one meetings are intentional and provide the environment conducive to growth. These meetings are best when the relationship between manager and colleague are at a high trust level.
- **High Potential colleagues:** Colleagues who demonstrate a unique level of commitment and competence have potential for larger roles within the organization. Mentoring programs for these colleagues can pay big dividends in the future.

Culture is your catalyst for organizational growth. As your team sees your commitment and intentionality to training they will identify as being part of a dynamic organization committed to continuous improvement. Training leads to competence, competence leads to confidence and confidence leads to consistent superior performance.

Colleague Development

Personal Development Plans

An organization is the sum total of all of its individuals. For an organization to achieve greatness, its individuals must achieve greatness. For individuals to achieve greatness they must continually improve their performance as they strive to achieve their full potential.

Napoleon Hill, the well-known success author, was quoted with the expression "A person cannot exceed mediocrity without the help of others". He understood that people need the help of others in order to realize their human potential. You are in the position of being able to help your team members far exceed mediocrity. In fact you are in a position to help team members achieve greatness.

You elevate your team members through training, coaching, encouraging, supporting and architecting personal development plans.

When it comes to architecting a colleague's personal development plan a manager must diagnose before they prescribe. Diagnosing an individual's developmental need is the result of observing their performance and receiving feedback from an array of stakeholders. This feedback process can be either spontaneous from day-to-day interactions or formal through outside agencies that provide an automated 360-degree feedback process.

Formal 360-degree programs require the colleague complete a self-assessment. Secondly, individuals such as the colleague's manager, peers, direct reports and other stakeholders will complete the same assessment.

A 360-degree feedback program provides an in-depth report of how colleagues score themselves in key competencies. Additionally, the report shows how the participants score the colleague in the same competencies. The findings of this data will highlight the colleague's competencies as either strengths or areas for development. The report also shows gaps in self-awareness where the colleague rates themselves significantly lower or higher than the group.

Once this data has been diagnosed the manager can now work with the colleague to prescribe their personal development plan.

When building a personal development plan consider these suggestions:

- **Don't Boil the Ocean:** You have the data that indicates competencies that are in need of development. The temptation is to fix every weakness, but the key to development is to pick the top two or three competencies and focus on them until positive change is recognized.
- **Define the Desired Outcome:** As you determine which competencies need to be improved, you and the colleague need to define what success looks like once the competencies have improved.
- **Regular Follow-up:** Competency improvement takes effort and intentionality. Regular discussion on progress to goal during planned one-on-one meetings is the ideal forum.
- **Heighten Awareness of Personal Growth:** Improving competencies should be viewed as a natural outcome from applied efforts. As you

support the colleague on their journey to achieve personal greatness it is beneficial to highlight the activities and efforts that will lead to improved competency. People do not transform overnight, rather it is a day-to-day micro-improvement that is easy to overlook. You can facilitate growth through your keen observation, insight and encouragement.

Personal development plans are valuable in your efforts to transform your organization. Remember that a person cannot exceed mediocrity without the help of others. You are the catalyst for transformation.

Personal Transformation Plan			
Development Focus	Why this Competency ?	Action Plan	Expected Outcome

Colleague Coaching

The success of your business will be equal to the aggregate success of your colleagues. With this premise it makes sense that your primary focus is to do everything within your power to energize your team and facilitate the accomplishment of their mission and goals.

The colleague coaching process is intentional. It takes dedicated time out of your schedule. Managers who commit to a consistent coaching process become advocates as they see the numerous benefits for the colleague, organization and themselves.

An important aspect of the colleague coaching process is to observe and listen. Consider visiting and observing the colleague in their work environment. Examples of this include:

- Traveling with a sales colleague and observing their engagement with customers.
- Visiting a construction project and observing progress, field conditions, work quality and safety conditions.
- Attending a service call and observing troubleshooting methodology of the service technician.
- Observing a system certification test or annual inspection.
- Reviewing the final design work of a systems designer or engineer.
- Shadowing administrative personnel to observe workflow and quality control process.

The first question managers should ask themselves is "What do I intend to accomplish?" There are multiple benefits that can be realized from planned colleague coaching engagements. You will learn how the colleague performs their work. Additionally, you will learn about the colleague's attitude, problem solving skills, customer skills, organizational skills and their professionalism. Beyond learning you have the opportunity to demonstrate your interest and care for the colleague. You can discover insights on how you can help the colleague and facilitate their success. In many cases this is the expression of genuine appreciation for their efforts and contributions.

In one respect, planned colleague engagement is the most impactful and rewarding part of your job. Great managers recognize the long-term value of regular coaching meetings and keep them as a priority in their schedule.

Do you believe that planned colleague coaching will benefit the colleague and the organization at large? If not why would you conduct them? The engagement should be focused on positive feedback however negatives are not ignored. As a rule 80% of your feedback should be positive in tone where 20% is constructive or dealing with corrective behaviors.

Colleagues must see the coaching process as a beneficial process to them. Consider how you view being the subordinate in a coaching meeting, do you feel energized by the experience? Do you feel the meeting lacked benefit or was de-motivating? It is your responsibility to make the coaching meeting constructive and valuable.

The colleague coaching process is a means for achieving your vision. Energized colleagues are central to any formula in achieving superior results and organizational greatness. You are the catalyst. Planned colleague coaching is the means.

One of the best practices for planned colleague engagement I witnessed was by John Ford, a service manager in Hawaii. John developed a practice where he would schedule Wednesdays in the field and visit job sites, service calls and inspections. John had conducted this routine for many years; consequently the colleagues were very comfortable with the presence of the manager in their work environment. A great deal of the John's communication was around the task at hand, inquiring if the colleague needed any assistance, and the expression of appreciation and encouragement. Most of these meetings then involved a brief customer meeting to check in, listen to concerns and express appreciation for their business. Not surprisingly, these meetings were overwhelmingly positive.

Planned colleague engagement is a high leverage process. You will energize your colleague, build a great culture and have fun while you do it.

High Potential Programs

In your perfect world you build a culture of continuous improvement and your colleagues continue to develop into peak performers. Furthermore you hire in top talent that raises the bar for your organization. You have established your organization as the best of the best.

Although this is exactly your vision one reality becomes evident, your competitors are improving at the same time. Everyone must elevate performance to survive and thrive.

If like-minded leaders are all striving to improve their organizations what else can you do to separate your organization from the pack? The answer lies in the development of future leaders.

Every organization has a normal distribution curve of talent- high performers, competent performers and poor performers. On the leading side of the normal distribution curve are your peak performers. This group consistently demonstrates superior efforts, superior results and are respected by their peers and customers. Many of these individuals have high potential to take on greater roles and responsibilities within the organization.

The recognition that some colleagues establish themselves as promotable to higher positions of responsibility is not a revelation. What has become recognized is that managers have the ability to facilitate the development of high potential colleagues thereby preparing them to step into larger roles with confidence.

You may ask, what was wrong with the traditional approach of baptism by fire? It certainly molded many great leaders. But how many potential successes were thwarted because of circumstances where the new leader was not fully competent for the challenges presented. When a colleague has high commitment but low competence to the task they need a directive style of leadership. More commonly, they are given a delegating style of leadership. They are being set up for failure.

Having a High Potential Program provides the means to prepare colleagues for many of the predictable challenges that lie ahead.

The objectives of the High Potential Program include:

- **Colleague Retention:** Many top performers are career ambitious. They aspire to progress within the organization or move to challenging assignments outside their current company. You recognize the value they provide and realize they would be difficult to replace.
- **Recognize Value:** When individuals are recognized for their contributions they naturally feel a sense of pride and appreciation. Self-esteem grows. They are motivated to make future contributions.

- **Determine Career Aspirations:** Many colleagues love what they do and want to continue on in their current capacity. Others want career advancement. The High-Potential Program helps clarify options and timing of best-next moves.
- **Build a Personal Development Plan:** The plan for a high potential colleague will be robust. It includes outside training courses, mentoring programs and special assignments.
- **Build Confidence and Competence:** The program exposes colleagues to the common duties and challenges of their future role. Competency in a new role can only be gained with repetitions but exposure to the challenges of the role is intended to excite the colleague for the future promotion. Participation in the program will instill confidence in the colleague. They will realize that you believe in them and their ability to learn and grow.
- **Succession Planning:** As your organization evolves you will inevitably need new leaders due to attrition or expansion. Your High-Potential program is directly linked to your succession planning process.

When building the developmental plan for your High Potential colleague there are several elements that should be included:

- **Assessment:** Evaluate the colleague's performance. Determine the key competencies vital for the future position. Build a plan to develop these competencies.
- **Mentoring:** Assign a mentor who will impart valuable thoughts, attitudes and advice to the

colleague. The mentoring relationship is for a finite period of time.

- **In-Job assignments:** Special projects expose how colleagues respond to change and challenges. Remember to utilize the appropriate leadership style.

The High Potential Program is a tool for organizational development. It is a benefit to both the colleague and the organization if both commit to the extra work required.

Mentoring

Developing your organization requires focus, passion and the cooperation of many allies. Although you are the critical "x- factor" in successfully developing your organization your efforts alone will not suffice. You need the assistance of others. One widely accepted approach in colleague development is the utilization of mentors.

Mentoring relationships can play an important role in the development of your organization. The objective of establishing mentoring relationships is to facilitate colleague development. Human development is a personal project and although organizations can facilitate training and development only the individual can realize their potential. The colleagues are ultimately accountable for their own development.

Mentors serve an important role in the acceleration of your organization's development. The key roles of the mentor include:

- **Trusted Advisor:** A source for advice from an experienced colleague.
- **Confidant:** An individual who is trustworthy and non-judgmental.

- **Coach:** An individual who can provide coaching and feedback.

Although the mentor and the mentee do the heavy lifting of the mentoring program your leadership in the program's success cannot be overstated. Most colleagues that are introduced to the mentoring concept for the first time do not know what is expected of them. By the same extension most mentors do not know the expectations placed upon them when first solicited.

To get the most out of your mentoring program consider the following:

- **Define the Objective:** By crafting a program objective with a set of guiding principles you will set the tone for the life of the mentor/mentee relationship.
- **Collaboration with Mentors:** The underlying purpose of the mentor is to facilitate the development of the mentee. There is a trust relationship that must be honored between mentor and mentee. Consequently, you must receive appropriate feedback that allows you to best influence growth.
- **Solicit Feedback from Mentees:** The objective of the mentor/mentee process is for the mentee to accelerate their development. An effective means of holding the mentee accountable for their development is to have them provide a feedback report of what they are learning through the mentor.
- **End Date:** The formal program should have a beginning and end date.

The mentoring relationship is organic. It naturally develops based on the chemistry of the mentor and mentee. The relationship must be one of mutual benefit that generates energy between both parties. The role of the mentor is to facilitate colleague growth.

Great mentoring programs require effort by you and the participants. Ultimately your leadership commitment to the program will result in organizational growth.

Business Partner Development

Imagine the following scenario; you have developed your vision of the future. You have a well thought out business plan completely aligned with your department managers. The plan has been communicated with the team and they are energized to serve your customers. Results are surpassing your expectations. Current staffing is working overtime to keep up with demand. You evaluate the situation and determine that recruitment and development of new colleagues will not provide a timely enough solution. What can you do?

This scenario is actually very common. When stars align and the economy is robust demand for products and services can outstrip supply. Great managers have a plan for increasing capacity beyond their internal resources and traditional recruiting. <u>The solution is outsourcing.</u>

Common labor elements that may be outsourced include:

- **Installation Labor:** This is the most common form of outsourcing. Many organizations have their own internal installation departments. When backlog grows and internal resources cannot respond timely to meet completion dates subcontractors become a welcome option.
- **Electrical Work:** Many low voltage companies do not perform licensed electrical work such as conduit and power. When prime work opportunities present themselves you will need to hire a subcontractor with the appropriate licensing, bonding capability and insurance.

- **Specialty Contractors:** There are situations where it is better to hire a specialist rather than have your resources self-perform work. Some examples include:
  - Scaffolding
  - Painting
  - Door hardware
  - Trenching
  - Fire watch
- **Project Management:** Although you might think subcontracting project management would be odd, it has been done and has been effective.
- **Engineering and Design:** It is beneficial to have relationships with several low voltage designers. Most markets have small design firms that are cost effective and responsive.
- **Specialty Engineering Services:** Some examples include structural engineers that calculate load-bearing forces to ensure the appropriate mounting hardware is used. Another example is seismic vibration testing of control panels.
- **Intra-company Resources:** Regional, national and international companies have the opportunity to share resources. This is often a win-win situation when one office has a high demand and another office has excess supply.
- **Manpower Services:** When a project demands additional labor and the long-term need is uncertain the utilization of manpower service is a viable option

- **Friendly Competitors:** Managers typically oppose using a competitor but I have had positive results with this tactic when in dire straits for manpower.
- **Interns:** Engaging young talent is another low risk and cost effective way to acquire resources while evaluating talent and cultural fit.
- **Consultants:** Specialty knowledge is occasionally needed to effectively accomplish project requirements. Consultants can play an important role in project execution.
- **Product Partners:** Technology partners have many resources that can improve efficiency and support project execution. Some of the services that may be offered include; design, programming, technical support troubleshooting, training and commissioning.

Outsourcing provides leverage for your business. Some managers have a philosophical bias. They believe they must self-perform all work. Although reasonable, there often comes a time when subcontracting or outsourcing becomes a better solution.

Every outsource option relies on building a contractual and business relationship. It is advisable to be proactive and build relationships with key partners before urgency and crisis hits.

Assess Progress

The astute manager is constantly assessing the development of their organization to understand what is improving, what is not improving and the factors affecting change. Your top priority is the support and development of your management team. Developing your management team requires consistent assessment of their progress.

As a busy executive you must be efficient. One of the tactics to managerial efficiency is to establish a consistent cadence and rhythm to the way you assess progress, provide feedback, manage expectations and lead change.

Consider the following methods of assessing your management team's progress:

- **Weekly Managers Meeting:** Manager meetings are a means for you and the managers to share important information that guides decisions. Regardless of the format and tone of the meeting you will determine a great deal about your management team's competencies. Over time the development of the managers will become evident by the way they prepare and participate in these meetings.
- **One-on-One Meetings:** The second means of assessing progress occurs during regularly scheduled one-on-one meetings between you and your direct reports. The agenda of these one-on-one meetings is predicated on current priorities. It is typical to review your direct-reports progress on

major projects, progress on key metrics and their personal development goals.

- **Quarterly Business Plan Updates:** On a quarterly basis your managers should present their business plan progress review. During this meeting the manager highlights their progress to goals, analyzes what is working well and what needs shoring up.
- **Year-end Assessments:** Year-end assessments are often viewed as the ultimate progress assessment. These reviews are beneficial to reflect and learn about the business environment and how the commitment and competency of the individual contributed to their department's success. The assessment provides guidance in establishing next year's goals.

Set Goals

Managers are keenly aware of the importance of goals. The intensity and focus around the achievement of financial goals is the most obvious. Equally important are the developmental goals and activity goals that when achieved will facilitate the accomplishment of greater financial goals.

Developmental goals refer to improving competency in knowledge and skills directly related to the job assignment. Activity goals refer to effort and efficiency.

It is widely agreed that goals create the roadmap to success. Written goals that are reviewed regularly and shared with others have a high probability of attainment. You can support the achievement of your colleague's goals by keeping them as a focal point in your weekly one-on-one meetings.

The goal setting process can be motivating and rewarding for both the colleague and the organization. You are the master architect that aligns organizational objectives with colleague goals. When done correctly, colleagues will recognize their meaning, purpose and benefit.

One common formula used when creating a goal follows the acronym of **SMART**, which means they must be:

- **S**pecific
- **M**easurable
- **A**chievable
- **R**elevant
- **T**ime Bound

By ensuring goals follow this criteria you and your colleagues will experience greater clarity that should lead to greater success in goal achievement, The SMART goal formula works!

An organization that has a culture of creating and aligning goals and then driving for their achievement is destined for greatness.

Section 6 - Develop Leadership Team Excellence

Align Our Belief System

Achieving your vision of organizational greatness requires the commitment and effort of many colleagues. Additionally, it requires leadership, both the personal leadership of each colleague and organizational leadership of your management team.

Strong leadership is essential in achieving your vision. Strong leaders will have a high degree of variability in attitude, philosophy and approach. All of which will affect the culture of your organization.

Harnessing the collective energy of your team requires that you value and encourage the unique talents of the individual while establishing a set of core values, attitudes and beliefs. When you align your leadership team improved results will follow. One key area of alignment is leadership philosophy.

Leadership Philosophy

The first statement when developing your leadership philosophy is "What I Believe". A central belief for you and your management team is servant leadership.

Servant leadership is a leadership philosophy in which an individual interacts with others with the aim of serving and supporting. Great leaders promote the well being of their colleagues. You must practice servant leadership to your direct reports. In return your direct reports must practice servant leadership with their direct reports.

The management guru, Ken Blanchard has spoken and written extensively on the subject of servant leadership.[21] Decades of self-serving leaders have hurt the world. Blanchard saw the need for something better that resulted in his philosophy of servant leadership.

Quoting Ken Blanchard "The most effective leaders are good human beings; they care about people, they listen more than they talk and they help people win". Can you align your leadership team around this philosophy?

Shared Vision

You have established your vision of the business. You know what you are building and why. You can envision how great the future state will look and feel for colleagues, clients and community. Can you imagine how much more enjoyable and successful the journey will be if your leadership team shares your vision and are as passionate as you in its attainment?

Aligning your vision is no simple task. It would be irrational to think that everyone would jump on board to accomplish your vision at its pronouncement. Think about how you respond when someone provides you with their vision of the future. Do you embrace it immediately or do you challenge the logic and benefits of the vision?

There is no doubt that having a shared vision is a huge differentiator in the timeline for success. Here are a few practical suggestions on creating a shared vision:

- **Share your Vision:** As the leader of the organization you are steering the ship to a destination. Colleagues want to know where the ship is heading

---

[21] Ken Blanchard, *Servant Leadership, YouTube Video*

and what is the destination. What is your vision? Colleagues join organizations for various reasons; compensation, career growth, work assignment and company stability. Many colleagues are compelled to join because of a leader with a vision.

- **Explain Your "Why":** Sharing your vision is a starting point but most people need a bit more. Why is the achievement of your vision important? Colleagues should logically be asking "What is in it for me?" Connect the dots for people as to how the accomplishment of the vision is good for the colleagues, clients, Community and the organization.

- **Ask for Involvement:** Making your vision a reality requires the effort of the entire team. Ask your teams or departments to collaborate and develop their vision statements that support and align with your organizational vision. This has proven to be an effective exercise that creates higher levels of engagement.

- **Reinforcement:** Communicating your vision is not a one-time thing. It is literally an everyday thing. Although you might not articulate your vision statement daily it should be mirrored in your actions and the actions of your leadership team. The critical mass of colleagues, when asked, should be able to state what the vision is and their role in achieving it.

- **Report Progress:** Achieving the organizational vision is a multi-year journey. Like any journey you need to assess progress and determine if you are on course, on time and if there are any obstacles down the road. This is analogous to achieving your business vision. Your team needs to know how they are tracking on the journey. Give them regular feedback.

Every consideration listed above is the responsibility for every member of the leadership team. When you and your team are aligned great results will follow.

Commitment

Commitment is an attribute that is admired when we see it demonstrated. A leadership team that is aligned in their commitment to achieving goals is powerful. Commitment encompasses the key elements of effort, ethics, work/life balance, creativity, courage and belief.

- **Effort:** Leaders are being observed and evaluated by their followers. This is a benefit to leadership when it comes to setting the tone for work effort. Leaders should never expect their team members to give greater effort than they personally exert. Leaders who set the tone with great effort are establishing the cultural norm of the organization. Effort is a critical piece in achieving results. All champions believe their effort is the key to their success. Effort is the input that leads to the output result. The leadership team must be aligned in their expectations of each other as servant leaders.

- **Ethics:** Achieving goals are gratifying. As goals get progressively more challenging individuals can become compulsive in their achievement. This behavior can be inspiring especially when leaders are celebrated for leading organizations to notable accomplishments. The desire to achieve goals at any cost is where many managers have lost their leadership opportunity. Having a burning desire to win is inspiring, but winning must be done the right way. In your role you are responsible for driving financial results. This includes recognizing cost within the appropriate financial reporting period, billing to contractual terms and booking contracts that meet organizational standards. Every member of the leadership team must remain objective and transparent.

- **Work/Life Balance:** Many managers would proclaim that work/life balance is one of the greatest challenges in growing organizations. I would agree. Understanding that leadership positions are demanding, individuals who sign-up must accept the reality that they "own" their business. It is not a 40-hour a week job. You are on 24/7. This does not mean you are convicted to hard labor. It does mean you have to figure out how you architect a high performing team and culture that performs their duties with a high level of autonomy. Business life is demanding and can be stressful. Naturally, everyone must have respite outside of their work. The leadership team must recognize this and support each members needs. Business success is but one aspect of our life's mission.

- **Creativity:** You and your team will be faced with business problems that must be solved. As your business grows so does the size of your problems.

The leadership team must be aligned on how they approach challenges that will inevitably arise. Leaders we must be analytical with risk assessment and positive in their search for best solutions.

- **Courage:** The leadership team must be transparent and honest with each other. Great leaders encourage members to offer different perspectives. The entire team must express their views with confidence. It is an accepted view that <u>none of us are as smart as all of us</u>. Have courage to use your voice. Have courage to keep an open mind.

- **Belief:** The leadership team must be aligned in their belief of the vision, mission and strategy. They believe in the organization, the management team and themselves. They believe they will deliver results. They believe that when the game is on the line they will make the play. They believe in the mantra "If it is to be, it is up to me".

A leadership team with a shared belief system is powerful. The belief in servant leadership, a shared vision and a commitment to deliver results will achieve organizational greatness.

Maximize Trust

In his book *The Seven Habits of Highly Effective People,* Steven Covey breaks down trust into two dimensions, trust of character and trust of competence.[22] Picture some of the people you have worked closely with in your career. How did those individuals that you trusted most measure in character and competence?

Character

When discussing the character of an individual I am referring to the moral qualities that define the person. Some of those qualities include integrity, ethics, honesty, courage, generosity, loyalty, compassion and kindness. People who rank high in these qualities are referred to as having a moral compass, meaning their moral standards are oriented on a fixed point that helps keep them on track.

To determine the character of the members of your leadership team you must observe them over time and in various situations. When you meet someone for the first time you have no basis to determine an opinion of his or her character. But immediately you begin to evaluate and measure individuals based on their words, actions and appearance.

Over time your perceptions are reinforced or modified based on observation and feedback. You develop a

---

[22] Steven R. Covey, *The 7 Habits of Highly Effective People, (Simon & Schuster, New York, 2004)*

paradigm of the individual based on patterns. You believe you can predict how the person will behave in situations. You trust that observed character traits from the past would be displayed in future. The premise that you can trust a person to consistently demonstrate a character trait does not suggest that the trait is of the highest moral standard; it just means you trust how the person will behave.

The objective of developing leadership team excellence is to be excellent. Excellence suggests that character must be of the highest moral standard. As leaders we must trust that each member of the leadership team is striving to live by the highest moral standard.

Achieving the highest moral standard is a bit nebulous. How do you measure the highest level of integrity? Rather than measuring character traits of team members in absolute terms you need to discuss perceptions and specific behaviors. From there, an action plan to improve upon negative behaviors is recommended.

The expression "We measure others by their actions, we measure ourselves by our intentions" is relevant in this discussion on character. It's easy to assume that most people believe themselves to be of high character because it is their intention to be of high moral standard. But their actions may betray them. It is your responsibility to provide honest feedback to your leadership team that will facilitate growth toward excellence.

Competence

Assuming you and your leadership team rank high in character you have half of the trust equation locked down. The second component to achieving trust is high competence. Think of individuals in your life that rank high in character, but if asked to perform a task that is outside of their competency they would be ill equipped to perform the task. Your trust is not complete. You trust their character but not their competence.

All managers have some competencies that they are very strong in while other competencies need improvement. Measuring the overall competence of an individual manager or the team at large might look like a sliding scale that attempts to aggregate many skills into a composite.

All businesses likely need to improve manager competencies. The starting point is always with assessing the current state. For managers this starts with doing a competency assessment. One of the common products utilized is the 360 Review. Armed with this assessment knowledge a personal growth plan can be created that will result in improved competency in the most opportune areas.

Your business is complex. Because of this reality the competencies required of the leadership team must expand and adapt. As competencies improve so does trust.

Confidence

You and your leadership team shared vision and determination to achieve organizational greatness. You must have the right mindset to accomplish your goals and objectives.

As you and your leadership team learn and grow you expect consistent improvement in character and key competencies. You will get improved results in the areas that you place your focus. You must place focus on the most important character traits and competencies. Understanding that human change is gradual, have patience and remain persistent on managing change within yourself and the leadership team.

It is important that you connect the dots for your team. Provide regular communication updates on how the input activities are causing output results. Unless you highlight the change in character or growth in competencies your team may not be aware of their progress. Change is often unnoticed until reflected upon over time. By reflecting upon your management team's growth frequently you can accelerate growth in both character and competence.

As character and competence increases so does trust. As the character and competence of the collective leadership team grows so does the ability to consistently deliver results. Consistency breeds confidence.

Maximizing trust is a key lever in achieving leadership team excellence. Trust is the highest form of human motivation. A highly motivated leadership team is unstoppable.

Set Expectations

Every manager has expectations. They have expectations of themselves, expectations of each member of their leadership team and by extension, every colleague within the organization. The questions I pose to you is:

- How well does your team understand your expectations?
- How have you communicated your expectations?
- Are your expectations formal or implied?
- Are your expectations reinforced regularly?

Expectations can be misunderstood and misinterpreted. They are formal and informal. Some are communicated well and reinforced while others are implied and loose.

One lever to develop your leadership team's excellence is to harness the power of expectations. Let's review how expectations impact culture, how you communicate expectations through your leadership philosophy and how goals and expectations support each other.

Culture

The leadership team is responsible to lead the organization to its vision. Sounds pretty simple. In reality, the achievement of your vision is so complex that one can only attempt to address the key elements. Clearly vision, mission and strategy are big rocks when it comes to business planning and leadership team alignment. But inherent within any successful organization is a culture that supports the values, beliefs and ideals.

A great leadership team understands the power of a strong culture and will make deliberate efforts to raise awareness with all colleagues. Colleagues gain this awareness through numerous means such as interactions with other colleagues, historic documents and on-boarding manuals. But the primary source comes from the leadership team through the formal sharing of expectations.

You and your leadership team are responsible for defining expectations. Let's review some key considerations.

Defining Expectations

Before you can express your expectations to your leadership team you must have clarity on what your expectations are. Expectations are a belief that someone will or should achieve something. That "someone" could be you, members of your management team or any colleague within your organization.

Expectations can be in the form of behaviors, activities, quality or productivity. The list of expectations can be incredibly lengthy. Think about your audience and determine the appropriate categories and quantity of expectations. Some examples of expectations include:

- **Behaviors:** Behavioral expectations include professionalism, attendance, attire, teamwork, work rules, reporting, and communication standards.
- **Activities:** Activity expectations include the number of client visits, number of site visits, conducting weekly staff meetings, and completing essential business functions by the requisite time and date.

- **Quality:** Quality expectations include conducting regular safety meetings, completing training and development exercises, conducting site audits, evaluating key metrics and demonstrating continuous improvement.
- **Productivity:** Productivity expectations include sales proposal pipeline volume, booking performance, revenue and margin performance, number of service calls per day and field labor utilization.

The expectations you set will impact the culture of your organization. By defining your expectations and effectively communicating them you are setting the tone for behavior, effort and results. Setting the right expectations is essential. If the expectations are unreasonable you risk losing the hearts and minds of your team. If the expectations are too low you will not establish a high performance culture.

Communicating Expectations

You and your leadership team have many tools to communicate expectations. Some of the most common include:

- Annual business plan
- Performance reviews
- Written correspondence
- Presentations
- Verbal discussions

One additional approach to accomplishing this task is through the development of your leadership philosophy. I recommend you obtain the book *The Leader's Compass* by

Ed Ruggero. [23]Within this book you will learn the purpose, benefits and mechanics of writing your leadership philosophy. Defining expectations is a key component of a leadership philosophy.

When developing their leadership philosophy the leader will want to answer the following prompts:

- **What I Believe:** What are your beliefs around life and business? What is important to you? What do you stand for? How do you believe the world works?
- **What You Can Expect From Me:** How will you manage and lead the team? Remember that you are telling the team that they can hold you accountable for these expectations; furthermore you are asking that they challenge you when they see inconsistencies.
- **What I Expect From You:** Tell your team your expectations. Set the tone for the organization. Be clear in your communication.
- **My Non-Negotiables:** Define the behaviors or circumstances in which a colleague will be terminated in absolute terms.

Once you and the members of your leadership team have completed this document it is intended that it be shared in an appropriate and wise manner. Your leadership philosophy is a powerful communication tool. From first hand experience I can attest that sharing your leadership

---

[23] Ed Ruggero, Dennis F. Haley, *The Leader's Compass,* *(Academy Leadership, King of Prussia, PA, 2005)*

philosophy with your team will have a positive impact. When each member of your leadership team creates their leadership philosophy and shares it with their teams the impact is a force multiplier!

Goals

Goals are one form of expectations. Setting goals motivates us and excites us to want to push ourselves to grow. That is exactly the feeling you want every member of the leadership team to have as you set ever increasing goals for the organization.

Being a leader within an organization is a privilege and a challenging responsibility. As your organization matures and develops its competency it becomes confident in its ability to deliver results. But just as the team has become competent and confident in delivering on expectations, higher goals and expectations must follow.

A leadership team with a shared philosophy about growth expectations will be unstoppable. The team accepts that growth is mandatory. Consequently the leadership team puts all creative energies into achieving expectations. A leadership team aligned on expectations and committed to their attainment is on their way to achieving organizational greatness.

Learn and Grow

You and your leadership team are well on your way to achieve team greatness. You are aligned with a shared vision. Your mission is clear. You have a strategic plan in place. You trust the character and competence of your managers and you have aligned your thinking on expectations. Your business is progressing as expected and you recognize that you cannot become complacent. You must build capacity to prepare for the future and that starts with you and your leadership team.

The leadership team must learn and grow intentionally. In a previous chapter I presented the 70/20/10 model of learning. This is where 70% of learning happens through on the job experience, 20% occurs through mentoring/coaching and the final 10% is the result of formal classroom training.

It is evident that formal classroom training is an intentional learning activity. Mentoring and coaching can also be intentional, although in some instances the mentoring and coaching may not have that appearance.

The "Big Rock" opportunity is the on-the-job experience learning. Most learning is occurring day to day through human interactions and the inherent need to solve problems. It is difficult to consciously recognize all the things we are learning real time but with intentionality you and your leadership team can heighten awareness and accelerate the process of learning and growing.

You are responsible for developing the team and preparing them to meet the future opportunities and challenges. You are the architect. You must envision what needs to be built, that is, what skills and knowledge your team needs in order to compete. Here are some of the means and methods that can be utilized to facilitate learning and growth of your leadership team:

- **Assess Current State:** The adage that you must diagnose before you prescribe is an absolute. You must continually assess the strength and weakness of the team, both individually and as a group. There are many external assessment resources that are useful and uniform for example the Lominger 360. You may also build your own assessment tool that focuses on the competencies you believe are of greatest importance.
- **Develop a Plan:** Once you have assessed the team and its members you must determine how to develop critical competencies. Remember that the plan can be built around any or all of the learning methods of on-the-job experience, mentoring/coaching and formal classroom training.
- **Execute the Plan:** If you are the architect then your leadership team is the builder. They must execute on the plan by following the instructions, performing learning activities, internalizing its intent and completing on schedule.
- **Leadership Style:** It is beneficial for you and the leadership team members to master the application of Situational Leadership. Remember to apply the appropriate leadership style of directing, coaching, supporting or delegating based on the commitment

level and competency level of the colleague as it relates the development task.

- **Feedback and Coaching:** We all need feedback to understand how the world interprets our actions. Your team leaders need to be objective, constructive and supportive when providing feedback. The team relies upon and trusts your coaching advice. Feedback is most beneficial when provided closest to the behavior being assessed. This supports the practice of one-on-one coaching sessions. Regular feedback sessions build a rhythm. Progress can be documented and reviewed over time to see the impact activities have had on results.

- **Inputs Lead to Outputs:** When you think of a manufacturing process you can visualize the input of a raw material into a machine that processes the material and transforms it into a product. The input is raw material the output is a finished product. This transformation process is analogous to human development and team development where the input may be reading, classroom training, mentoring, coaching or job experience and the output is knowledge and competency. Once you determine the desired output think creatively to determine the inputs required.

- **Creative Thinking:** The expression "What got us here, won't get us there" is a reminder that we need to change. To change requires us to have new thoughts, new choices and new actions. By formalizing the creative thinking process you are making an intentional action to challenge the current state. You are taking the first courageous step to give up something good with the expectation of something better. Commonly referred to as "brainstorming", the leadership team collaborates over a problem statement with a plethora of potential solutions. These potentials are then stratified through a selection process that identifies the <u>best bets</u>.

- **Facilitate Change:** To change is to grow. Most people are not active change-agents so it often requires an outside force to drive change. You are that outside force.

You and the leadership team are on a journey to build something epic. See it in your mind's eye and clarify it with great detail. To achieve greatness the organization must get better, bigger and stronger. It starts with you and the leadership team. With a leadership team focused on learning and growing, excellence is inevitable.

Win Games

Developing leadership excellence is your primary means to achieving organizational greatness. Consider two questions; How do we measure organizational greatness? How do we measure leadership excellence?

Achieving organizational greatness is an overarching goal that stems from your vision, mission and objectives. This BIG goal is a multi-year journey that is tracked and measured by Key Performance Indicators (KPIs). Common KPIs include:

- Financial performance: Revenue growth, gross margin growth and profitability.
- Free cash flow.
- "Best-in-Class" efficiency metrics compared to the industry.
- Customer satisfaction ratings.
- Colleague satisfaction ratings.

Measuring leadership excellence parallels the Key Performance Indicators of organizational greatness. Common measures include:

- Achievement of financial goals of revenue growth, gross margin growth and profitability.
- Achievement of free cash flow goals.
- "Best-in-Class" efficiency metrics.
- High customer satisfaction ratings.
- High colleague satisfaction ratings.

Achieving organizational greatness can only be achieved through leadership team excellence. Leadership team excellence is measured by delivering results the right way and consistently winning in your chosen marketplace.

Winning at endeavors that are important to you creates euphoric feelings as well as a sense of pride from the accomplishment. Winning at overwhelming challenges builds an unstoppable confidence.

For the sake of analogy, think of your business fiscal year as a twelve game season. Each fiscal month is a game. Much like the NFL the pressure to win is very real. You need to prepare and perform at the highest level in order to win games. The scoreboard is your financial performance.

Great leaders know they must find a way to win. Giving their best effort is not the win. Achieving goals and objectives is the win.

Maximum effort and intense desire do not guarantee success in every game. The variables in business are numerous. Looking at your business as a twelve game season validates that you can come up short on a game or two and still make it to the playoffs. You need to position yourself to win the BIG game, to achieve your goals and objectives.

Winning games is essential to the development of team excellence? Winning teams become consciously competent, they believe in their abilities. Their confidence in delivering results is absolute. Consider some the additional outcomes of winning:

- The team is energized and optimistic.
- Stress is reduced while joy and happiness expands.
- Camaraderie and team spirit are enhanced.
- Team confidence grows.
- The business builds momentum.

- The culture grows stronger.
- Team members bond together and increase trust.
- The team continues to learn, grow and improve.

You and your team won't win every game. If you did it might indicate your goals and objectives are not challenging enough. An occasional setback is not a bad thing if you learn and grow from the situation. As the leader of your organization you help your leadership team cross the chasm in the way they view their responsibility and accountability in winning games.

As a point of caution, winning can become addictive and all consuming. You must ensure that winning is done ethically and complies with business guidelines. This is specific to revenue recognition and accounting principles.

You and your leadership team will undoubtedly face obstacles, setbacks, adversity and defeat. Although you would not invite these challenges, when they present themselves you must embrace them and confront the reality that you must overcome and fight to win the next game. These moments in time are formative for you and your leadership team's toughness and resilience. Focus on winning.

You have a vision, mission and strategy. Trust the plan and adapt as necessary. When your team wins games make it a point to celebrate. Show your appreciation and reward success.

You and your leadership team are building a championship culture. The team's confidence is growing. You are on the cusp of Achieving Organizational Greatness.

Overcome Adversity

Imagine a business where everything seems to flow smooth. Growth is easy. Achieving goals are easy. No customer issues, no human resource issues, no manpower issues, no cash collection issues. You name it, everything works. This actually sounds like the vision every leader would like to realize. But alas this never will happen.

Problems will always occur, and the bigger your organization becomes the bigger your challenges will become. Expect adversity, it is coming!

You can't predict the type of adversity or the time adversity will occur. But you can prepare your attitude and the attitude of the leadership team to embrace the challenge once it presents itself. Adversity is a serious opponent. If you handle adversity correctly the positive outcomes can be incredible. Handle it wrong and careers will be negatively impacted.

Here are a few perspectives on adversity and the role it plays in developing leadership team excellence:

- **Managerial Courage:** There are many types of adversity and the response will vary by situation. Each situation will require some form of managerial courage. Adversity will require you to act. Each situation will develop your competence and confidence. With confidence you will have the managerial courage to act decisively.

- **Objectivity:** When you and your team are faced with adversity you must look at the situation objectively and assess the situation.
- **Plan Response:** Once the situation is assessed you and the leadership team must develop a comprehensive response plan.
- **Unified Approach:** You and the leadership team must bond together to overcome the challenge. You are all in it together.
- **Attitude:** It is critical that the leadership team be aligned with a shared belief that they will prevail. Poise and confidence go far in removing fear from the masses.

You can't be sure of how your leadership team will respond to adversity until that bell rings. But history reveals that when a team is faced with adversity and comes out victorious they will experience a transformation in their confidence and beliefs.

Here are a few recommendations on how to prepare your team for the future:

- **Develop Managerial Courage:** You and your managers make numerous decisions daily. Each situation provides the opportunity to demonstrate your decision quality. Some of those decisions will be met with disfavor and opposition. Each of these situations will prepare you for future adversity and related response.
- **Build Leadership Culture:** Start with writing and sharing your leadership philosophy. When articulating, "What you can expect from me" you

can state your commitment to deal with adversity timely, courageously and innovatively.

- **Instill Next level Confidence:** Your team came to their positions with a base level of competence and confidence. Through your leadership you elevate their confidence to a new level. You instill the belief that they will overcome any challenge. They have the courage, the plan and the support to overcome any and all adversity.

Overcoming adversity is to taste greatness. Once a team has tasted greatness they are changed forever.

Section 7 - Achieve Organizational Greatness

Be The Catalyst

In the previous section I presented the formula for developing Leadership Team Excellence. The elements include:

- Aligning Beliefs
- Maximizing Trust
- Setting Expectations
- Learning and Growing
- Winning Games
- Overcoming Adversity

The successful application of these elements will move you and your leadership team closer to excellence.

This formula is simple, but its accomplishment is not easy. It requires a force to move the process along. It requires a catalyst. That catalyst is <u>you</u>.

By definition, a catalyst increases the rate of reaction. In your world you are the catalyst to increase the rate of growth, productivity and effectiveness of your organization. You are the catalyst that enables your leadership team to achieve greatness.

Let's review some of the roles and responsibilities that you have as the leader:

- **Role Model:** We all want to respect our leaders and to learn from them. You are the role model to your leadership team. You are always being evaluated for your commitment and competency. You need to bring your <u>"A" Game</u> every day.

- **Teacher:** As leader you are responsible for guiding the development of your leadership team.
- **Coach:** All teams need a coach. As coach, you organize efforts, provide direction and instill confidence. You create the playbook for the players and guide them to success.
- **Facilitator:** Business and life are full of roadblocks. You provide the service of guiding your team around roadblocks and help them achieve results in the most efficient manner.
- **Counselor:** Life's challenges can wear down the strongest of individuals and cause them to make questionable decisions. You provide a balanced perspective that will direct or redirect colleagues on a path to success.
- **Energizer:** You are the catalyst leader. You bring energy into the room when you enter. You are the catalyst for an energized leadership team.

Within theses roles you shape your leadership team. You must be great at these roles. You must be the most powerful catalyst.

To become the most powerful catalyst consider some of the following recommendations:

- **Align Beliefs:** The first step in aligning beliefs is to state what your beliefs are.
  - Start by creating and sharing your leadership philosophy with your leadership team.
  - Have each of your leaders create their leadership philosophy and share it with their teams.

- Collaborate with your leadership team and develop your mission statement and core values.
- **Maximize Trust:** You must earn the trust of your team. You are being measured in trust of your character and trust in your competence. At the same time you are measuring your leadership team. To maximize trust it starts with you being of highest character and highly competent. Some of the means of maximizing trust include:
  - Be congruent with your words and actions. "Walk your Talk" regarding your leadership philosophy.
  - Provide clear expectations with timely and specific feedback to leaders.
  - Conducting regular one-on-one meetings with leaders focused on their development and career progression.
  - Allow only positive comments and discussions about managers who are not present. Negative comments and gossip will destroy trust.
  - Apply the situational leadership skills of direction, coaching, supporting and delegation.
- **Setting Expectations:** Leaders are often frustrated and disappointed when the organization fails to achieve results. Unfortunately, it is often determined that expectations were not clearly defined or communicated but rather assumed to be

understood. Consider the following when setting expectations:

- Ensure the leadership team understands your leadership philosophy.
- Utilize the proper leadership style for the task.
- Provide consistent and timely feedback.

- **Learn and Grow:** The better your star players become the better the team performs. Partner with your leadership team in their development to achieve excellence. Techniques you may employ include:

    - Provide annual performance reviews to review strengths and areas of development of your leaders. Define specific development goals that are most relevant for career progression.
    - Conduct a 360 review of the leaders to gain comprehensive assessment of leadership competencies. Use the information to develop a personalized plan for improvement in key competencies.
    - Invest in outside leadership development programs for your leadership team to develop specific skills or to enhance self-awareness.
    - Conduct regular one-on-one meetings with individual leaders with a focus on development and improvement.

- **Win Games:** Winning games build confidence. You are the catalyst to achieving wins in several ways:

- Facilitate strategic thinking and the development of the business plan.
- Instill a sense of urgency within the leadership team. Demonstrate the importance of making and keeping commitments.
- Organize creative problem solving workshops that will generate ideas and solutions.
- **Overcoming Adversity:** Adversity can propel or destroy. With you as the catalyst it will propel. When the organization is faced with adversity you can serve as a catalyst in the following ways:
  - Set the tone through your calm confidence. Fear can destroy organizations. Leaders must conquer fear.
  - Guide the management team to develop a response plan to adversity. Confront reality, assess the situation, develop a plan with contingencies and take action.
  - Stay engaged and communicate progress. Successfully overcoming adversity is the only option.

In order to achieve organizational greatness you must develop your leadership team to excellence. Leadership team excellence will only be realized through you. You are the catalyst.

Sustained Energy

Achieving organizational greatness requires the collective effort of all of your colleagues for a sustained period of time. To apply sustained effort requires sustained energy.

Consider the sustained effort required of a marathon runner. They start the race well rested, hydrated, and fueled with the proper nutrition. They have the expected energy to begin the race. As the race progresses and the miles and hours accumulate the runner begins to fatigue. To boost and sustain energy they ingest water and some form of carbohydrates. This process is repeated numerous times throughout the race all with the goal of achieving the objective of winning the race.

In your "business marathon" you must be prepared to apply sustained effort. Your leadership team and all colleagues must be prepared to apply sustained effort. But for anyone to sustain effort they need fuel to harvest energy.

How does the human body activate energy? Without getting into quantum physics we have a basic understanding that our cells are likened to mini power plants that create energy from the fuels we provide in the form of food, water, air, sunlight, movement, sleep and thoughts.

Energy is the power required to do virtually everything. With optimal energy you are powerful! Your mental and physical capacities are working in lockstep. When your energy levels are low or depleted, you feel lethargic; your desire to work is compromised. In order to serve the world and to accomplish your life's mission you must have energy.

The benefit of having energy may be better described by its inverse, that is, "Fatigue makes cowards of us all." You have meaningful work that needs to be accomplished and being fatigued impairs your ability to achieve your cause.

There is abundant information on how the various fuels work to create energy; Consider the following fuels that increase your energy levels:

- **Food:** Fuel yourself with nutrient rich foods from nature such as vegetables and fruits. Eat organic. Eliminate refined sugars. Eliminate GMO foods, Avoid processed foods.
- **Water:** Water is essential hydrating and detoxifying our body. The quality of your water supply matters. Drink purified water when possible.
- **Oxygen**: Focused breathing techniques will increase oxygenation that will support mental and physical functionality.
- **Sunlight:** The sun provides vitamin D and is an essential source of life energy.
- **Exercise:** Our cells respond to exercise by repairing and strengthening muscles and body functions. Stress your body through regular exercise.
- **Sleep:** Your body needs time to recover and rejuvenate. Your brain must process the day's events.
- **Thought:** You become what you think about. Energy follows thought. Positive and constructive thoughts increase energy. Negative and destructive thoughts drain energy.

- **Meditation and Prayer:** Regular meditation and prayer can aid in bringing perspective and balance to the important things in your life. It also can reduce stress. Stress is an energy drain; so managing stress is a net energy gain.

The expression "It's simple but it's not easy" applies to this list of recommendations. In your quest to achieve greatness you will make regular sacrifices. You will give up sleep to maximize work hours, you may eat on the run and consume convenience foods, and you may skip exercising because of the fatigue of long days. I encourage you to be mindful that you have the power to increase your power. With self-awareness and education, you can make these fuel sources a catalyst for increasing and sustaining energy. On the flip side, abuse or inattention to these fuels can lead to fatigue, and consequently, sub-optimal performance.

As leader, you have a vested interest in sustaining the energy levels of your team members. Think about an army of soldiers fighting in war. They must have sustained energy. When in battle they have no time to eat or sleep but this can only be sustained for a limited time. They must get adequate rejuvenation with sleep, water, food and supplies.

Your team members need the same care and balance to sustain them through their "business marathon". In his book *The 7 Habits of Highly Effective People*, Steven Covey talks about the concept of <u>production</u> versus <u>production capacity</u>. As an analogy he refers to the fable of the goose that laid golden eggs. [24]As the story goes a farmer came

---

[24] Steven R. Covey, *The 7 Habits of Highly Effective People, (Simon & Schuster, New York, 2004)*

upon a goose that laid a golden egg, he was delighted and confused by this. When the following days presented the similar result he became more excited and delighted. Then the farmer became greedy and wanted more golden eggs immediately and decided to cut open the goose to get more golden eggs only to find no golden eggs and now a dead goose.

In this story the golden eggs are the production and the goose is the production capacity. In your business, the colleagues are your production capacity and they produce the results. You have a vested interest in your production capacity (colleagues). You have the wisdom to protect your colleagues and ensure they are energized. Energize your team members through the following actions:

- **Invest in Their Development:** Developing colleague skills and knowledge will increase production capacity.
- **Celebrate Accomplishments:** Recognizing and rewarding great performances will increase enthusiasm and self-esteem.
- **Show You Care:** Tune into your team members. Understand what is going in their lives and support them appropriately.
- **Keep Work Fun:** There are plenty of challenges that require intense effort. Find ways to reduce stress and keep things in proper perspective.

You have the privilege and responsibility to be the leader of your organization. Use your knowledge and disciple to maximize your energy levels. Use your wisdom and caring to maximize the energy levels of your team members.

Infuse Confidence

Great organizations have confidence in the capabilities of their colleagues and leadership. They are confident in their ability to deliver results.

Great leaders understand the impact confidence has on individuals, teams and organizations. Consequently great leaders take action to infuse confidence with intentionality. Leaders understand that they must infuse confidence in themselves and then their colleagues. Let's examine self-confidence and building colleague confidence.

- **Self-Confidence:** Self-confidence is earned. The expression "Fake it until you make it" is an acknowledgement that many individuals are on their personal journey to acquire self-confidence. All leaders must pay their dues. Day by day leaders develop their confidence through trial and error to the eventuality when they know they have achieved absolute self-confidence.

    It is a difficult task for a leader to infuse confidence into their team when they themselves are lacking self-confidence. To be clear, every person has some areas that they need to develop. This reality does not prevent a leader from being confident in their ability to lead. They are confident in their ability to solve problems through the time, talent and resources of others. They understand their strengths and weaknesses and they are savvy on how they confront reality. The formula for building confidence starts with taking action and tackling problems. Consistently overcoming problems builds competency in your management and leadership skills. Consistency then leads to confidence.

- **Building Colleague Confidence:** Imagine what your organization would look like if all colleagues lacked confidence to perform their assignments. Very scary. Imagine the organization when every player has supreme confidence in their ability to complete their mission? Very powerful. In reality all organizations teeter in the middle. Leaders understand that the majority of team members have moments of high confidence and moments of low confidence. This can be related back to the situational leadership model defined by Ken Blanchard.[25] As a refresher, your leadership style must match the development level of the colleague for the task they are required to perform.

Development Level		Leadership Style	
D1	High Commitment Low Competency	S1	Directive
D2	Variable Commitment Some Competency	S2	Coaching
D3	Low Commitment High Competency	S3	Supportive
D4	High Commitment High Competency	S4	Delegating

---

[25] Ken Blanchard, Margie Blanchard, *Situational Leadership II, 1985*

In example, a colleague required to complete a task that they have previously demonstrated competency on would be expected to have high confidence. Their manager should apply a "delegating" leadership style. This would infuse greater confidence.

An example of a poor application of situational leadership is when the colleague has low competence in the assigned task and their manager applies a "delegating" style of leadership. Most colleagues would be under high stress in this situation. This would not infuse confidence.

Expect that there will be times when your team members will lack the competency and confidence required to accomplish a mission. This is where your leadership will be required. At these times you must devise a solution, communicate the plan and utilize the appropriate leadership style to facilitate colleague confidence and ultimate success. The additional benefit is that success breeds greater confidence.

Get Better

In order to deliver better results individuals and organizations must improve. They believe in the adage "What got us here won't get us there". They embrace the principle of continuous improvement.

As leader of your organization you have the most significant impact on your colleagues. Your words and actions have great weight. Your leadership philosophy will guide the direction of your team. Your philosophy of continuous improvement will affect the momentum of your organization.

Your organization's growth is the result of both the improvement of each colleague and the team synergies. Masterful facilitation of colleague improvement and synergy is a key competency. The following practices will help your organization get better.

- **Leadership Philosophy:** Your leadership philosophy document is an ideal forum to communicate what you believe. Continuous improvement is essential to achieving organizational greatness. Spell it out and communicate it with passion.
- **Walk your Talk:** Colleagues are evaluating your actions for congruency or contradiction to your message. Ask yourself; how have I gotten better today? What have I done to improve myself intellectually, physically and spiritually?
- **Conceptualize Your Plan:** The mantra of "Get Better" must be followed with the plan of how you intend to accomplish this ideal. It is up to you to

build your program and determine the roles and responsibilities of all colleagues.

- **Communicate Your Plan:** A great plan is worthless if not effectively communicated to the colleagues. You are competing for your colleague's mindshare. Effective communication techniques, repetition and reinforcement are essential.

- **Inspect What You Expect:** Colleagues are accountable for their own development. Colleagues have the best intentions to accomplish their developmental goals but urgent and important events often compromise their intentions. Great leaders understand that colleagues become consumed by business urgencies. To aid colleagues great managers instill processes to monitor the progress of individuals and teams. Your insight, encouragement and facilitation are essential. You are the primary source of momentum.

- **Connect the Dots:** It is difficult to gauge daily improvement in absolute terms. Leaders help connect the dots for colleagues and highlight how their development efforts will lead to future output results. Getting better starts with the development of knowledge and skills that will be applied in future situations.

- **Utilize Operational Excellence Tools:** Many organizations have benefitted from the implementation of formal operational excellence programs with the intent of reducing waste through process improvements. Two notable methodologies include Six Sigma and Kaizen. Both of these methods require the expertise of trained individuals to lead programs to success. Absent a trained leader, there are many analytical tools that can be implemented intuitively that will drive improvement.

You are building a culture of continuous improvement. Your plan is working and momentum is building. Keep getting better!

Develop Mental Toughness

Your colleagues will face moments when they feel overwhelmed. The timing of customer demands is out of your control but the commitment to serve your client's needs is the mission that must be accomplished. In these situations it is expected that your colleagues will rise to the occasion and deliver the necessary results.

Extreme customer demands tax the limits of colleagues, as do numerous internal demands such as meetings, reporting, training and project reviews. All of these demands add to the daily pressures.

Managers face many of the same pressures plus the burden of scheduling, human resource issues, executive reviews and financial management tasks.

Leaders have many demands that are time sensitive. Additionally they have personnel issues and business performance issues that are urgent. When leaders have more urgent demands than they have time the outcome is stress. Stress is an internal mechanism that puts your brain on high alert. Psychologists refer to this as the "fight or flight" reaction. As leader, you have no choice but to stand your ground and fight the stress situations.

Where does mental toughness fit in? Mental toughness can be described by the following traits:

- **Focused:** The ability to partition critical issues from non-critical.

- **Objective:** The ability to look at the situation and confront reality.
- **Problem Solving:** The ability to evaluate situations and their associated risk and develop options for optimal resolution.
- **Poised:** The ability to demonstrate calm confidence that the resolution will be achieved successfully.

Even the best of leaders can have breaking points where the challenges are overwhelming. It's a difficult place to be but it is ultimately where confidence and courage manifest themselves. Challenging events can either destroy or develop individuals. Leaders have no choice but to self-develop and embrace the moment.

To achieve organizational greatness requires more than mental toughness by the leader, it requires a critical mass of colleagues to be mentally tough. So what can you do as leader to develop mental toughness within the ranks? Consider the following:

- **Demonstrate Mental Toughness:** As situations present themselves demonstrate focus, objectivity, problem solving and calm confidence.
- **Apply Situational Leadership:** Provide the appropriate leadership style for the task based on the colleagues commitment and competency level. Directing, coaching, supporting or delegating.
- **Encourage and Inspire:** Your genuine encouragement and concern will fuel colleagues. They will not want to disappoint.
- **Learn and Grow:** Review challenging situations as a "lessons learned" discussion. What did the

colleague learn? What did they do well? What could be improved? What would they do differently?

- **Appreciate and Celebrate:** The pain experienced during epic challenges can be brutal. The resulting rewards of the challenge must offset the pain. Victories call for celebration. Let your team feel your appreciation.

An organization with a shared attitude of mental toughness will overcome all obstacles. You are the catalyst for building a culture of mental toughness. Model the way and lead your team to greatness.

Deliver Results

Your objective is to achieve organizational greatness. Sounds exciting but how do we define organizational greatness and then determine its attainment? In the introduction of this book I presented the model of personal greatness that is comprised of five elements. They are:

- Maximum Effort
- Hero Principles
- Continuous Improvement
- Serve Others
- Deliver Results

Your organization is the sum total of all of your colleagues. The achievement of personal greatness by each of your colleagues will result in the achievement of organizational greatness.

As leader your challenge is to deliver results. You can only deliver results through the time, talents and efforts of your colleagues. You must strive for 100% of your colleagues achieving personal greatness. So how do you approach this challenge? Here are some recommendations:

- **Spark Excitement:** Many colleagues have not thought deeply about achieving personal greatness but given the spark by trusted leadership many will align their thinking and adapt behaviors.
- **Reinforce:** Your colleagues are bombarded with messages and data. Capture mindshare by reinforcing the message with power and repetition

until the colleagues accept and associate with the principles of personal greatness.

- **Culture:** Sparking interest and reinforcing the message are essential elements in making the vision of personal greatness a part of your culture. It takes energy to build momentum. Once a colleague tastes greatness, they want more.
- **Model the Way:** You are the catalyst. Colleagues need to see you as the shining example of achieving personal greatness. Your effort sets the pace. Your principles inspire. Your commitment to personal improvement is evident. Your service to colleagues and customers is admired.
- **Educate and Align:** Not all colleagues connect the dots in the same way. You must clarify what the concepts of maximum effort, hero principles, continuous improvement, serving others and delivering results mean.
- **Encourage:** Your words have great weight and impact. Positive encouragement goes a long way to reinforce good behavior. Conversely, expressing your disappointment is impactful to changing negative behavior.
- **Synergy:** An individual working in a vacuum does not lend itself to achieving team greatness. Colleagues must recognize that team greatness requires harmony and alignment. Teams must go through a predictive growth process of forming, storming, norming and performing. As your organization matures stress is reduced and team greatness accelerates.

- **Assess Progress and Set Goals:** Achieving Personal Greatness is an individual journey. You play a significant role as coach. Napoleon Hill is credited with the quote "A person cannot exceed mediocrity without the help of others". You have a significant impact on helping your colleagues achieve personal greatness. As coach set SMART goals and provide feedback to help colleagues attain personal greatness.

Rome was not built in a day nor is achieving personal greatness. Success is predicated on the performance of all colleagues. Use your wisdom and insight to position your colleagues for success. Once a critical mass of colleagues achieves personal greatness outstanding results will follow.

Believe

It is common for a motivational speaker to encourage their audience to <u>dream big</u>. One example phrase is "What would you do if you knew you could not fail?" That catch phrase can cause us to pause and wonder about the possibilities of our life.

Conversely one often sees the hurdles and barriers in life. The prospect of achieving challenging goals can overwhelm one's sensibilities.

Where does your mind land? Are you the optimist or the pessimist? Are you wearing rose-colored glasses? Is the glass half empty or is it half full? Are you focusing on absolute success or the possibility of failure?

The power of your thoughts and beliefs are absolute. In the introduction of his book, *As a Man Thinketh*, James Allen offers the following poem:[26]

Mind is the master-power that molds and makes,

And man is mind, and evermore he takes

The tool of thought and, shape what he wills

Brings forth a thousand joys, a thousand ills

He thinks in secret, and it comes to pass,

Environment is but a looking glass.

Many years ago I read a news story that depicts the power our thoughts have on our existence. This is the article:

Paramedics recently removed the frozen remains of a railroad worker who was unfortunately locked inside a

---

[26] James Allen, *As a Man Thinketh*

refrigerator car. The train was setting its couplings prior to departure from the station when the door to the refrigerator car unexpectedly slammed shut, trapping him inside. Toward the end of the train's 300-mile journey, the trapped worker succumbed to hypothermia. The man chronicled his last hours of life in great detail on a clipboard found near his body. He described each moment of the chilling, numbness until finally losing consciousness.

Officials who read the man's last words described the event as a painful tragedy. What made the man's death even more tragic was that he was trapped inside a refrigerator car that was out of service due to a broken inside latch and a faulty cooling system. The refrigerator unit was turned off. The temperature inside the car never got below 47 degrees.

According to the medical experts, the man literally imagined himself freezing to death until it became a reality, even though his body temperature never actually lowered to the point of freezing.

Psychologists say that the human imagination is so powerful that depending on how vividly we can imagine, things can appear 60 times more real to us than they actually are.

I would submit to you that what the experts say about the power of our imagination is correct. The human mind is indeed powerful, yet if our minds can so dramatically and vividly imagine the negative, it seems logical to me that the reverse can be equally powerful. (Author-unknown)

Our minds are powerful. We will achieve what we believe. Reflect upon your belief system and battle any thoughts that are counter-productive to your vision. Remember, we become what we think about.

Take Action

This manual, the Greatness Guide for Managers, is the playbook for achieving organizational greatness. It provides information and ideas that could prove beneficial on your journey. But the only way information can become a benefit is if it is acted upon.

During my career I recall moments when I gained an insight from another individual. One of those moments came from Tom Peters in his book *In Search of Excellence.*[27] When researching great companies he found one key attribute was a <u>bias for action</u>. A mantra that one of the great companies used was "Do it. Try it. Fix it." The premise being that all the ideas and knowledge are meaningless if not acted upon.

Knowledge without Application = Nothing

Think of a scenario where the playbook of the current NFL Super Bowl Champions fell into the hands of another team. Would the possession of that information cause the other team to win the next Super Bowl? Not likely. The result of winning a championship requires more than good information. It requires effective execution.

All championship teams have a coach who aligns, unites and leads the charge. You are the catalyst. You set the pace. You lead the charge. Your sense of purpose and urgency to achieve the vision is clear and present every

---

[27] Tom Peters, *In Search of Excellence*

moment. There is a direct cause and effect from your action or inaction. Consider the following:

- **Prioritize Your Actions:** You can do anything but you can't do everything. Achieving your vision is a multi-year journey. Plan your moves accordingly.
- **Demonstrate a Sense of Urgency.** Be the example for your team when it comes to respecting the use of time, making and keeping commitments and holding self and others accountable.
- **Model the Way:** You are the living, breathing example of "taking action". Your team will follow your lead. Start by demonstrating your personal leadership.

Your leadership provides the spark to ignite your entire organization. It is your job to use your spark to fan a flame. Your passion and insight will lead your colleagues in the direction to success. But you cannot achieve personal greatness for them. You are building momentum with the critical mass. Your daily actions should be focused on facilitating greatness throughout the organization. Take action today.

The days, weeks and years are fleeting. Time is your fiercest opponent. Act with a sense of urgency today and everyday and remain focused on Achieving Organizational Greatness.

Achieve Organizational Greatness

7. Achieve Organizational Greatness
6. Develop Leadership Team Excellence
5. Increase Organizational Capacity
4. Manage and Improve Processes
3. Build an Energized Team
2. Build and Execute Strategy
1. Build Leadership Foundation

Final Thoughts

Achieving organizational greatness takes the collective superior efforts of every colleague. But it all starts with you, the leader. You are the catalyst. You lead the way. Your mantra: "If it is to be it is up to me".

Wishing you the best of luck on your leadership journey. May you have many great challenges and even greater accomplishments.

"If it is to Be it is up to Me"

Achieve Greatness

Bernot Best

The mission of Bernot Best is to lead, serve and teach organizations and their key colleagues who are engaged in the low voltage industry.

Bernot Best was founded with the vision of helping clients be the best they can be. We focus on developing personal leadership, business acumen, strategic planning and management skills. We approach this through creating customized transformation plans that define key development objectives, collaborate on a desired end state and build a program map to deliver the result.

Andy Bernot is the President of Bernot Best. He began his sales career in the low voltage industry in 1982. He has held leadership positions for the past 30 years.

For information on how Bernot Best can support your quest to achieve personal greatness, team greatness or organizational greatness you can contact us via email at andy@bernotbest.com

References

1) Napoleon Hill, *The Law of Success, pp. xxi (The Penguin Group, New York, 1928)*

2) Steven R. Covey, *The 8th Habit, (Simon & Schuster, New York, 2004)*

3) Steven R. Covey, *The 7 Habits of Highly Effective People, (Simon & Schuster, New York, 2004)*

4) Ed Ruggero, Dennis F. Haley, *The Leader's Compass, (Academy Leadership, King of Prussia, PA, 2005)*

5) Ed Ruggero, Dennis F. Haley, *The Leader's Compass, (Academy Leadership, King of Prussia, PA, 2005)*

6) Jim Horan, *The One Page Business Plan, Independently Published 1998*

7) Steven R. Covey, *The 7 Habits of Highly Effective People, (Simon and Schuster, New York, 2004)*

8) Steven R. Covey, *The 7 Habits of Highly Effective People, (Simon and Schuster, New York, 2004)*

9) Jim Horan, *The One Page Business Plan, Independently Published 1998*

10) Robert B. Miller, Stephen E. Heiman, *The New Successful Large Account Management, (Business Plus, New York, 2005)*

11) Ken Blanchard, Margie Blanchard, *Situational Leadership II, 1985*

12) F. Jon Reh, *(Understanding a Company's Culture, The Balanced Careers, May 9, 2019)*

13) National Training Laboratories, Bethel, Maine

14) Napoleon Hill, *The Law of Success, pp. xxi (The Penguin Group, New York, 1928*

15) Napoleon Hill, *The Law of Success, pp. xxi (The Penguin Group, New York, 1928)*

16) Ken Blanchard, Spencer Johnson, *(The One-Minute Manager, 1982, Publisher William Morrow)*

17) Jim Horan, *The One Page Business Plan, Independently Published 1998*

18) The Proski ADKAR Model

19) Bruce Tuckman, *(1965) Development Sequence in Small Groups, Psychological Bulletin*

20) Ken Blanchard, Margie Blanchard, *Situational Leadership II, 1985*

21) Ken Blanchard, *Servant Leadership, YouTube Video*

22) Victor Frankl, *Man's Search for Meaning, (Beacon Press, 1959)*

23) Steven R. Covey, *The 7 Habits of Highly Effective People, (Simon & Schuster, New York, 2004)*

24) Ed Ruggero, Dennis F. Haley, *The Leader's Compass, (Academy Leadership, King of Prussia, PA, 2005)*

25) Steven R. Covey, *The 7 Habits of Highly Effective People, (Simon & Schuster, New York, 2004)*

26) Ken Blanchard, Margie Blanchard, *Situational Leadership II, 1985*

27) James Allen, *As a Man Thinketh*

28) Tom Peters, *In Search of Excellence*